Networking and Mentoring
A WOMAN'S GUIDE

Dear Chio,

I hope this may help and inspire you.

Love Maura
xx
x

⑤ $3.50

Networking and Mentoring

A WOMAN'S GUIDE

Dr Lily M. Segerman-Peck

PIATKUS

© 1991 Lily M. Segerman-Peck

First published in 1991 by
Judy Piatkus (Publishers) Ltd.,
5 Windmill Street,
London W1P 1HF.

*The moral rights of the author
are asserted*

British Library Cataloguing in Publication Data
Segerman-Peck, Dr Lily M.
Networking and mentoring: A woman's guide.
 I. Title
 331.70082

 ISBN 0–7499–1065–8
 ISBN 0–7499–1055–0 pbk

Edited by Susan Fleming

Photoset by Wyvern Typesetting, Bristol
Printed and bound in Great Britain by
Bookcraft Ltd, Midsomer Norton, Avon.

To my life companions:

Catherine Peck, my mother
Irene Jones, my sister
Brenda Woods, my other sister
Pat Soberman, who opened the door

Contents

Acknowledgements

No book is ever written by one person alone. And no thought is the product of only one mind. I am constantly aware of how important other women are to my continuing development, and I acknowledge my debt to them for their companionship.

Most of the people who have shared their experiences with me specifically for this book have asked not to be named. I respect their wishes, but want to record my gratitude for the full and frank help they gave.

Indeed I have been overwhelmed by help. Even people I hardly know have sent me articles or references, sometimes as a result of a brief conversation on the phone. (What a wonderful networking instrument that is!) Working with women is truly wonderful.

A special thank you to all the female information scientists who helped me with my literature search, who said not infrequently 'I'm not really meant to be doing this, you know. . .' but who nevertheless found me the references I needed. Some even disappeared into back rooms to answer silent phones long enough for me to copy down what their computer search had thrown up on the screen.

And a very warm thank you to two writers. Eliza G. C. Collins sent me one of her last remaining copies of *Dearest Amanda*, the best text on mentoring in practice that I know. It is shortsighted of the English publishers (Collins) not to reprint it. And Tim Heald, author of *Networks: Who We Know and How We Use Them*, who, despite not knowing me, lent me a copy of an American text not available in this country.

Perhaps this is the moment to record that I have also received enthusiastic support from several men, who have shared their knowledge and aspirations with me. In particular I want to thank Ted James MA, Vice-President Marketing, of Consulting Resource Group, Vancouver, Canada, for stimulating conversations on many subjects.

Among the people I can thank by name are Jill Johnson of Mind Management whose contribution, though quantifiable, was immeasurable; Marion Devine who very generously shared her own research on mentoring with me; and Susan Fleming, who didn't quite know what she was taking on when she agreed to edit this book.

And finally I come to Women in Management. WIM was started 21 years ago by Eleanor Macdonald, MBE, BA, PHD, CBIM, FIPM, a woman manager at a time when this was almost a contradiction in terms, and an entrepreneur of substantial reputation. She is a trainer of international repute, and one of the most generous women I know. Eleanor has given freely of her time and experience, and has also introduced me to other women who have in their turn offered me their help. This is a perfect example of networking in action. I hereby acknowledge my considerable debt to Eleanor, and all those she put me in touch with. I also want to thank the Executive Committee and staff of WIM who publicised my request for information from women who had experienced mentoring. Networking with WIM members has always been a delight. May they think that their support has been worthwhile.

INTRODUCTION

Networking and Mentoring: Utilising the Human Resource

When I changed career eight years ago a book on networking and mentoring didn't figure on the list of things I planned to do. But almost everything that I have seen or done in my professional life since then has propelled me towards it.

For more than twenty years I have been involved in careers advice. I now offer courses and private counselling in career development, and about 60 per cent of my clients are women. A good many of my clients know where they are heading and come to me to brush up on specific skills which they know they will need if they are to rise further in their careers. Some come to discuss why they are not rising faster. Some are having real problems: I have been seeing more and more people who have been left to develop on their own without guidance from senior staff. In several instances indeed they have been suppressed or abused by their seniors. They are under-used as people, many of their skills not being used at all, and their growth, both personal and professional, has been stunted. I have some clients who have been almost brutalised by their experiences. Some have become aggressive or bitter. Some are close to despair. As one client put it to me: 'All I want is to get out from under.' What a waste of human resources.

My own professional life is generally considered to be successful, but at certain stages I encountered difficulties for want of guidance, and so did many of my colleagues and friends. When I started work I was left entirely to my own devices. This was not because I was obviously brilliant, but because it was like that. If you rose, you rose by your own efforts, rarely aided by senior staff. The merit of this system was that those who rose deserved to rise. But there were many who fell who could have become good if a helping hand had been extended at an appropriate stage.

I rose. But if I had been given a helping hand by a senior colleague I would probably have risen further and faster, and I would have changed certain aspects of my career much earlier than I did.

What helped me was that I had marvellous colleagues and friends. I had a whole array of people I relied on for personal and professional support, who also relied on me when they needed help of any kind, from the loan of a book, through hints with counselling techniques, to babysitting. And through them I met other people whose help I could draw on and who in their turn came to me. In other words I had a well developed network of people who were very important to my professional and personal growth and well being.

Being mutually reliant on people in this way was second nature to me, for I had been a student at a university where people were considered important. Keele was a pioneering university. It was notable, amongst other things, for the tutorial system it used. At the time such a system was rarely found beyond the walls of Cambridge or Oxford, from where indeed it had been imported, by Lord Lindsay of Birker, who had been Master of Balliol before becoming the first Principal of Keele. Each student belonged to a tutorial group, comprising not only five or six other students but also two or three members of the teaching or research staff. The students were all in the same year but studying different subjects, and the staff members were from a number of different disciplines broadly representing the humanities, natural and social sciences. Each student read a paper to that tutorial group and received critical comments from the others, staff and students alike.

I later went on to teach at the University of Manchester Institute of Science and Technology. My department also had a highly developed tutorial system, with each student being assigned two tutors, one to act as an academic tutor, the other as a personal tutor to help with matters of personal growth.

I thus learned early in my professional life that people are very important in the development of other people: the different perspectives of their various backgrounds contribute to the information on which an individual makes a decision or takes an action. I am now very adept at using other people, networking in other words, and can usually find someone who can help me with a task, or someone who knows someone else who can. I also spend a lot of my time teaching other people the importance of networking, since the solution to so many of the problems I come across can be found by meeting more people and learning from their experience.

What I have never had is a mentor. Which is pretty ironic, since I have acted as a mentor to many many people, men and women alike. Mentoring is a powerful system for making progress. It depends on the positive partnership of two people: a 'junior' partner, the mentee or protégé(e), who wants to get ahead and a 'senior' partner, the mentor, someone who is already ahead, who wants to help the junior learn the ropes. It is a system that has, for centuries, helped men to advance in their careers; but few women have been privileged to experience its effects.

Fortunately women are now finding that it can work for them too, women who have worked their way up the corporate ladder, and those who now own their own business. Kathryn Stechert Black has reported on the success of American business women who have had mentors, but in Great Britain we have our own successes: women like Jennifer d'Abo, best known for her time as chairman of Rymans; Sheila Needham who started as a secretary and now owns her own printing company; Sophie Mirman, mentored by Lord Sieff from Marks and Spencer, now bouncing back after the collapse of her Sock Shop empire; Linda Kelsey, formerly editor of *Cosmopolitan* magazine and now editor of *She*. But politicians too benefit from mentoring: Americans like Elizabeth Dole, Secretary of Labor in the Bush Administration; and Geraldine Ferraro, mentored by Tip O'Neill, Speaker of the House of Representatives for many years, who was chosen by Walter Mondale to be his Vice-Presidential running mate in the 1984 election against Ronald Reagan. In our own country, Emma Nicholson, the Conservative Member of Parliament and former Party Chairman, acknowledges the guidance of her mentors the Rt Hon Michael Alison MP and the present Speaker of the House of Commons, the Rt Hon Bernard Weatherill, MP.

But mentors can be helpful beyond the world of work: Sarah Knight went through a revolution in life philosophy and personal

13

values. She was an 'unemployed drifter' when she met her mentor; now she is highly paid, marketing computers. This book is based on research with women who acknowledge that mentoring has been an important factor in their progress, and who want to share their experiences with other women.

Although I have never benefited from mentoring, I have benefited from networking, both of them systems of utilising the resources of other people in making progress. Networking and mentoring are found in many different walks of life, but in this book we shall be concentrating on getting ahead at work. And here we mean *paid* work or employment. If this book were intended for men it would not be necessary to define these terms, since the work or employment of men usually results in money payment. But the reverse is true for women. Most of women's work in our society is unpaid, work as housewives, mothers, carers and voluntary helpers. Much of their work enables other people (usually men) to progress in paid employment.

But this book is intended for women: women who are themselves in employment, or who want or need to be in employment. It is intended for women of all ages, and at all stages in their career, from those who have not yet started, to those already in employment and seeking promotion, to those who are returning to work after a break. It is also for those who are wanting to change career, whether currently in employment or not.

Why am I writing a book for women on networking and mentoring? Very simply, to help women get on. I want women to get on because it gives them freedom of choice. For too long most women have been restricted in what they can do in their life because of financial dependence on a man, whether husband, father or brother. This dependence was actually encouched in our legislation up to recent times, and it wasn't until 6 April 1990 that women became entirely (legally) responsible for their own tax affairs. Financial independence and the power that it brings can be achieved by making progress in a career of your choice. The right to advancement in a good and interesting career should be a right granted in equal measure to men and women in our society. But it isn't. Women still come up against barriers at all levels in preparing for and practising a career. And that isn't fair. This book seeks to help put the balance right.

But I am also, let us be clear, writing this book ultimately to help society, women *and* men. We need a flexible and imaginative workforce to take us into the next century, with a range of skills and qualities to maintain and improve our standard of living. But in training and employment we largely discount the skills and qualities of half the population. For the future of our society, we cannot afford to go on doing this. It is particularly unwise to disregard the potential of women when we are facing that well-known demographic time-bomb, a drop in the number of school leavers, male and female, such that we are facing severe shortages of labour in certain areas. And we ignore at our peril the potential of the Single European Market which will not only allow our workers to work on the Continent, but will allow workers from elsewhere in Europe much freer access to jobs in this country. Will our workers be ready to meet the challenge of working on the Continent? Will our women? The answer to this last question may be, joyously, 'Yes'. For, of all the people graduating from polytechnics and universities in this country in modern languages, 75 per cent of them are women. So the women are ready for Europe in a very important sense. Now they need to reap the harvest of that readiness. For their own good, and that of our society.

What I had needed, and what my clients need, and what I am now providing for them, is a mentor. We could all do with a helping hand, someone who is prepared to help us develop, who will help us look at ourselves, assess our talents, our aims and our expectations (not the same thing), and help us move towards them, or even beyond them. As a client recently put it to me, when I was suggesting that she might look for help from someone senior in her company: 'But you're talking about a mentor, aren't you? There's no one in my company who is that interested in me. No one who will take that much trouble. You'll have to be my mentor.'

She is a woman. I am a woman. This book is about women, and is written primarily for women, though I have no desire to exclude men from my readership. Although I am very pro-women, I am in no sense anti-men. Indeed, I hope that men will find a few insights here. In particular I hope that they will learn how to encourage and develop and utilise the skills of women at work, for the sake of the women, for the sake of their companies, and for the sake of our society. Too much talent has been wasted already. With the

15

demographic time-bomb about to go off, we have no time left to lose.

So herewith my book on networking and mentoring, with not a little love to those who preceded me and those who will follow on.

CHAPTER 1

Why Women Need a Helping Hand

From the moment the sex of a child is determined, often nowadays before birth, that child is handled differently according to whether it is a boy or a girl. Not only is the physical treatment it receives from its parents and others different, but so are the assumptions about the role it will play in society. It is, for example, assumed that a boy child will grow up to work for a living, and he is prepared by conditions at home and in school to do this. (This is nowadays the norm also in aristocratic and even royal circles.)

The same cannot be said of girl children. Girls are still brought up in a climate where undue weight is given to their biological function, their ability to bear children. This biological function has traditionally been extended quite 'naturally' to encompass the social functions of child rearing, home-making and house work, and generally supporting and servicing a husband (or father or brother) who is economically active. In this system women are judged not to need any personal income as their requirements are met by their menfolk. Thus, even in this day and age, boys and girls, men and women, are socialised to conceive of a woman as a dependent and subservient being, whose best bet for happiness is to attract a husband who can keep her and their children in comfort if not in luxury. Hence the diverse nature of the compliments society still pays to children: boys are intelligent, girls are pretty.

This bit of social manipulation has been skilfully packaged for centuries as the 'natural' and 'proper' state of affairs, such that even decent, well-intentioned men have difficulty in regarding women as anything other than the smaller, hence weaker sex, who, having the propagation of the species as their primary role, deserve male support and protection. It is, of course, true that when an individual woman is carrying a child and for a while after the birth, she does need such support and protection, from everybody. But it is ingenuous to allow a women's need for support at such critical moments to justify not encouraging women to do anything other than stay at home propagating and rearing their young and providing decent accommodation. This is a convenient deceit, and deserves to be exposed for what it really is: a device for ensuring that women devote all their energy to supporting their husband and his career and not their own, and hence maintaining men in a position of power over women.

The consequences of this state of affairs are both ethical and practical: the restriction of decent earning capacity to only one half of our society is intolerable; and the preparation of only one half of our society for wealth-producing activity is economically unwise.

The situation is, of course, more complex than implied by the brief sketch above, for at various times in our history women have worked for wages, and particularly in recent years women have been entering a wider range of occupations in greater numbers. But the fact remains that women do not enjoy equal rights and privileges with men in employment terms. Women still earn significantly less than men, for no proven difference in ability: the average female salary is 75 per cent that of the male. Many more women than men are in part-time work, and consequently have fewer employment protection rights and reduced pension benefits.

This state of affairs has been changing, but for the good of the nation the pace of change must be increased. We do have legislation to deal with discrimination in employment, and we are now seeing national legislation being supported and advanced by European law. But legislation can only do so much. What is really needed is a fundamental change in attitude to women and employment. And this change is necessary in women themselves on the one hand, and those who train and employ them on the other. From the earliest possible moment girls must be helped to think of themselves as full members of our society who will work and be economically independent, for their own sake and that of their future partners and offspring. Why should men be obliged to support women financially, any more than women should be obliged to service men? At all stages women must take themselves seriously as wage earners. They must give more attention than women have done in the past to their possible life patterns, to see how paid work fits into the total context. They must give proper thought to their career options and choose their subjects at school or college with care. They must then apply for jobs which will allow them to meet their own life goals, rather than just accept what seems to be on offer. And when they are in employment they must behave in such a way that their employers know that they want and are suitable for promotion.

But such an attitudinal change can only come about if girls receive appropriate encouragement from the earliest opportunity. This means that parents, educators, trainers and employers must perceive girls as future wage earners and deal with them accordingly, giving them the same support and encouragement as they do boys. They must provide them with the same opportunities as boys to study all subjects, and in particular those which are important for employment purposes, including maths and computer studies. They must cease to think of certain activities and careers as more suitable for men than women and cease to restrict women's choices. More than this, they must actively encourage girls to expand the traditional female horizons. For the sake of the next generation, and the next. . .

Equally employers, and at the moment these are mostly men, must be helped to see women as workers, as colleagues, as employees who have a serious potential to help their business grow. They must stop seeing women just as wives, mothers, daughters, etc. who, if they work at all, are a source of unskilled casual labour, and prepared to work only for pin money. I have heard this phenomenon described as 'female blindness'. Employers look straight through women colleagues as if they do not see them. They must learn to think of women as serious contenders for jobs and careers. Some employers are enlightened enough to appoint women, but even then they have trouble considering them for responsible positions: only 27 per cent of the supervisory and managerial posts in Britain are held by women; 4 per cent of senior managers are women, and only between 1 and 2 per cent of really top management jobs are held by women (figures from NEDO, December 1990).

I see the same thing repeated in public bodies, those committees like industrial tribunals, health authorities, consumer and arts councils, whose members are appointed by Ministers to advise on or carry out government policy. Approximately 23 per cent of the members are women, but fewer than 1 per cent of the bodies are chaired by women. As recently as spring 1990 I was phoned by a male civil servant who asked me to search my databank of women and to put forward someone suitable to chair a large public body, a position with a high level of responsibility and corresponding remuneration. This was shortly before they wanted to make an appointment, and he apologised for contacting me so late in the day. Hoping no doubt to forestall criticism, he made a denigratory reference to his own chauvinism. He didn't help himself by going on to say, 'It just didn't occur to me that we would find a lady suitable to do the job.' I decided that a dignified but piercing silence was the most appropriate response. The point of this story is that this man had the responsibility for bringing forward to a Secretary of State names of people capable of doing the job required. Yet he very nearly ignored half the population in his trawl.

As I write I am still smarting from the failure of the new (male) Prime Minister to appoint any women to his Cabinet, despite the example of the past eleven years in which a woman was the *leader* of the Cabinet. The usual well-founded rumour has it that he *did* ignore the Conservative female Members of Parliament in his trawl. That seems just about to sum it up. For it cannot possibly be the case that he considered all Conservative women MPs and decided that they were *all* inferior to some of the men he actually appointed. Not malice. Just limited vision.

At the moment we have two tasks. In the long run we must attempt to change attitudes and procedures so that future generations of women will be adequately treated and helped to take a full place in the world of work. But for the immediate future we must help those who have grown up under the old régime. Such women are about to make job or career choices. Or they are already in employment, facing difficulties of advancement. For them we must try to counteract the failure of their years as a child and young adult to prepare them adequately for the world of work. And for the failure of our system to enable men to see women as colleagues to be taken seriously.

Some progress has already been made. We now have legislation which outlaws discrimination against women in education and employment. More importantly, this legislation actually allows us to discriminate in favour in women: there is a specific provision of the Sex Discrimination Act of 1975 to allow training provision to be made for women only, to enable them to be compensated for missing out earlier. And we also have campaigns and organisations, like WISE (Women into Science and Engineering), WIT (Women in Information Technology), the 300 Group Educational Trust, and the Roadshows of the Women's National Commission, which are trying to overcome inadequate educational provision. For, as a friend of mine put it, 'Otherwise, we don't have the opportunity to take advantage of equal opportunities under the Act.'

Hennig and Jardim, in their excellent book *The Managerial Woman*, hit the nail on the head when they compared the plight of women entering the world of business to someone travelling abroad and encountering a culture of which they have no experience, for which they have had no preparation, but which they must nevertheless learn to handle if they are to survive (pp184–186). There are a number of things we can do to help women learn about this new culture like directing educational projects towards it, arranging work shadowing, having more businesswomen in the press and media (particularly television) to provide role models, etc. But one of the most potent things we can do for women about to enter this foreign country, or already floundering there, is to provide a guide, someone who has lived there for a while, is quite at home there, knows the rules, knows the pitfalls, who will interpret and advise, etc. This person is, of course, a mentor.

What is a Mentor?

The term 'mentor' is ancient. It comes from the original Mentor of Greek mythology. Mentor was a friend of Odysseus who chose him as the tutor of his son, Telemachus. Since that time 'mentor' has been used to describe a teacher, tutor or guide for life. In the 18th and 19th centuries it was used in the title of books which were to guide you in certain areas of learning, like medicine or naval arts.

I came across a delightful work in the British Library called *The Female Mentor*. It was published in three parts between 1793 and 1796 when feminist stirrings were beginning to be felt, by one

Honoria, who 'is unknown to the world and wishes to continue so'. It is a collection of texts to supplement the work of Amanda, the mother of numerous offspring, who led a discussion circle for her children. So popular were these that others wanted to join in. There were too many actually to join the circle, so Honoria published the volumes, 'based on TRUTH and NATURE, intended to promote the cause of RELIGION AND VIRTUE'. The title derives from a comment made by one of Amanda's children: 'Indeed, madam, I will always follow your advice, for you are our *Female Mentor.*' The texts themselves are very revealing, accompanied by one or two tongue-in-cheek comments from Honoria. She notes for example that she has had deliberately to collect together the texts about significant women in history, for they are otherwise overlooked! She also states her disappointment at finding so few women worthy of inclusion, but 'The recollection, however, that very few opportunities offer, which ought to call women into action, and that their greatest merit consists in not being known, in some measures relieved my disappointment' (pp121–123). *Plus ça change. . .?*

The term 'mentor' has again become fashionable in the last fifteen years or so, particularly in North America, where mentoring has expanded rapidly as a system of management development. Much of this is a formalisation of the successful mentoring reported in organisations like the Jewel Companies, where three consecutive chief executives formed a mentoring chain to groom successors (see Collins and Scott).

This has given rise to many articles on mentoring, most of them in academic publications. The *Annotated Bibliography* of mentoring texts, published in autumn 1989, lists 541 items which appeared between 1986 and 1989 (see Gray). In all it is reckoned that about 900 articles on mentoring have been produced since about 1975. Fewer than ten texts on mentoring in the workplace have originated in Britain. But a number of surveys have been carried out and reported (see PA Consulting Group, Clutterbuck and Devine, Industrial Society), and a major survey by Arnold and Davidson is in progress. Particular interest has also been shown in mentoring and its value for women (see Arnold, Lyles, Clutterbuck and Devine, Swoboda and Millar, Reich, *The Mentor Connection*), and the term 'womentoring' has been used by Hetherington and Barcelo (*qv*), to designate the mentoring of women. They also draw specific attention to the needs of 'women of colour'. Mentoring has also been used as a compensatory strategy for young people from the Black Community in Britain (see Chapter Seven).

Several of the academic texts discuss the differences between teacher, coach, counsellor, etc. For the purposes of this book, such detail is not necessary. A mentoring role can be taken by a number of people, a teacher, a neighbour, a senior colleague, even a parent, anyone who finds the talent in you and will help you develop it. Your mentor is your guardian angel. Someone who is knowledgeable, helpful, wise, prepared to help you along the path of your career, take you by the hand to help you over puddles in the road, catch you when you fall, and eventually give you wings to fly alone. The women who have helped me with this book have had one or more mentors at different stages in their life, and have needed them for different parts of their career journey. Most of them now mentor others.

To my mind the most important function that a mentor can perform for women at the moment is compensatory, to help women catch up on what they have missed out on, so that they can make proper progress. This makes the role of people mentoring women slightly different in detail from that of mentoring men, and we shall look at this in the chapter on *being* a mentor. For the moment let us look at the stages of a woman's career where having a mentor is helpful.

Choosing a Subject, Choosing a Career

Mentoring can start at school. While teachers or tutors are primarily reckoned to be instructors, passers-on of knowledge or a set of skills, the good ones help you develop habits of learning and thinking which you can apply far beyond the walls of a classroom. Teachers at school, college or university, or tutors on training schemes for the unemployed can thus act as mentors. If they are genuinely interested in you as a person they can help you see yourself in the context of the rest of your life and help you map out a possible future, seeing how employment fits in with other aspects of that future.

Let us exemplify this with a case very common amongst young women. The student in question is good at languages and discusses the matter either with her teacher or a careers adviser. It would traditionally be perfectly reasonable for either of them to suggest that she consider teaching. Teaching is normally regarded as a 'handy' career for women. It is an area of work traditionally accepted as suitable for women, so that the kind of pioneering struggle that a woman geological engineer would have to face is not anticipated. Also, teaching does have a number of advantages for women who want to take time out for a family, or to work part-time.

But a mentor would help this student to look much more deeply into the matter, and would help her to answer a number of questions not even normally posed for women students who are good at languages. For example, is she interested in a career in which she can rise and rise? If so, can she find such a career if she offers foreign language skills as her major job qualification? She could teach, become a translator or interpreter. But these do not lead to very high management positions. Being the head of a translation section of a large company is commendable, but it does not lead to a place on the board. Similarly, if the student expects to rise to be head of a school or take some other appointment in educational management, should she be trying to get there through the route of classroom teaching? Are there any teacher-training establishments that are better than others for people interested in educational management? And if she is interested in management, should she be looking at a university course in languages? Why is she not considering management studies? And most fundamentally of all, a mentor would help her to consider what else she is good at, besides languages, or what else she could be good at, given the chance to study other subjects.

There is nothing wrong with studying languages. The major problem is what else it cuts out. Only when the student has decided that her heart is really in languages should she contemplate doing a degree in languages. Even then she has to analyse carefully whether it should be only languages, or combined with maths, or politics. And then whether she wants to use her languages in a future job, and if so as a primary or subsidiary skill, etc. Would her future life-style guarantee her the chance to return time and again to the country of her language to maintain the high level of skill needed for various jobs?

If young female students were able to have this kind of incisive discussion about their future then fewer of them would find them-selves frustrated at having made the wrong choice earlier on. A mistake at this level is not irrevocable, but it is costly. A mentor could not guarantee that no such mistake would occur. But she would alert her mentee to the possibility.

Climbing Up

Women who are already in work and looking for promotion can also benefit enormously from having a mentor. In this example we shall look at someone well established in her career. She was an accountant in a national bank, in charge of a particular section. She had made a good career choice, wanted to stay in that kind of job and that kind of working environment, but wanted to make sure she progressed upwards, with increasing responsibility. Now in her early thirties, she had invested a good deal of time and effort (her own, and that of her husband) in getting properly qualified. She had completed her accountancy qualifications and was now doing her banking exams. The last thing she wanted was to be overlooked for promotion.

At the time we take up the story she had recently had a break of a few months to have her second child. Although she had experienced some emotional difficulty going back to work (worse than after the first child) she had coped and had even been given a promotion to her next grade shortly after returning to work. She had a problem with her immediate subordinate, the man who had been brought in to look after her work during her absence. Without consultation with her, he had been promoted into her old job when she was upgraded, and put on to her permanent staff. In particular it bothered her that her immediate junior and her immediate senior (also a man) were continuing the habit they had developed during her absence of regularly having lunch together or a drink after work. As a result of this she was being missed out in the chain of information essential to the smooth running of her section.

She discussed all this very frankly with her mentor. Her mentor was not from the banking profession, but she had sufficient ex-perience of human situations, work structures, reorganisations, and her mentee's personality and skills to be able to listen

25

knowledgeably and critically. Together they worked out a regular reporting procedure which made the subordinate keep his manager (the mentee) up to date. She also started occasionally suggesting to her boss that they might have a quick discussion about something over lunch, or after work, thereby disrupting a pattern of behaviour that could have been detrimental to the efficient working of her department.

But, although things got better in the short term, this experience had made her see the writing on the wall. Her boss was certainly not directly discriminatory, and would have been scrupulously fair in assessing her. But he would only assess her on the work that had been assigned to her. He could not assess her on the work that he had assigned elsewhere. This was the crucial point. It had become clear that a close relationship had grown up between the two men, a mentoring relationship in fact, which did not augur well for her future. The bank was at that time undergoing substantial reorganisation, and she suspected that her subordinate would soon be made directly responsible to her boss, and be asked to lead special projects. While she continued the routine work of her department, these special assignments would challenge him and give him a big opportunity to shine and prove his value to the bank, and make his suitability for a senior position in the restructured bank more obvious than hers. Her responsibilities were important, but not eye-catching. Her whole future, despite her acknowledged competence, would soon be brought into question.

After lengthy discussion with her mentor to see if she were over-reacting she decided to apply for better posts outside her own bank. She could have stayed and fought, asked for special assignments, proved her value, etc. But what would have been the point of the fight? What she wanted was not victory over a junior colleague, but promotion to a more interesting position, and that could be achieved more easily and less acrimoniously elsewhere. Again after detailed discussion with her mentor, she sent her cv to another bank. They were obviously impressed. They replied saying that they did not normally recruit from outside at the level of responsibility that would suit her, but they would nevertheless be interested in meeting her. They also wrote to the mentor asking her for a reference. Her mentor had known her for fifteen years, so was able to give a full, informative and critical reference. After further intensive discussion with her mentor she attended two interviews and was offered and accepted a post with better salary, better perks and better prospects.

The mentee would probably have got where she wanted to go on her own in the end. But by being able to discuss the situation with her mentor, she was able to get there faster, armed with a perspective beyond her own experience, and renewed confidence in herself and her skills.

This story also illustrates some advantages of getting promotion by moving out of one organisation and into another, but at a higher level. It is true that you have to learn a whole new way of working, a new company culture. But you bring to your new job a fresh perspective from another environment, so the new firm benefits on the one hand, and on the other you have a chance to demonstrate your competence to a new set of people, a whole new network. You also have the opportunity to learn and compare working practices, thus improving your judgement in operational matters.

This increasing experience is important when you want to move up the ladder again, either in the same firm, or by moving out to another company. You are not just developing a wider perspective. You are also uniting two sets of contacts, two networks. This is important from two points of view: you bring to your new post your old network, your old source of support, that you can use to the benefit of your new job, enhancing your value as an employee; and you are also, to use the jargon, increasing your visibility – you are being seen by people in the old job and in the new as someone on her way up. You are letting more and more people know what you are capable of. And this will stand you in very good stead for the next promotion. For the more people who know you are right for promotion the more likely you are to get it, inside or outside the present company.

It is, incidentally, usually financially advantageous to move about. People who stay put are invariably paid markedly less than those who have proved their market value.

Banging Your Head against the Glass Ceiling

Another category of women who can be helped by finding a mentor comprises those who have their head up against what has come

27

to be known as the glass ceiling. This is a block in promotion. It is a phenomenon which afflicts women at senior management levels, when they are typically in their mid-forties and older. They are competent women, quite happily climbing up the promotion ladder, who suddenly find that they don't get any further. They don't see the ceiling above their head, for they look right through it, see the rungs above their head, and see who is occupying the rungs above them. Invisible the ceiling may be, but effective nevertheless. They themselves are stopped dead by it. This happens to women who have worked right through and given long, continuous and loyal service, as well as to mothers who have had a career break. They know that they have gained the necessary expertise and consider themselves well-qualified for promotion to the next stage. But they are overlooked, quite often being overtaken by men junior to them, and possibly less obviously well qualified.

There are a number of problems here, and all of them can be helped by having a mentor. One problem concerns women's understanding of what being 'well qualified' means in promotional terms. They have been brought up to believe that if they follow the rules they will be rewarded for good behaviour (promoted). In a sense this is true. But no amount of competence and good behaviour will help you if you don't follow the *right* rules for promotion. And the rules for promotion change as you go up the ladder. A mentor can do a lot to help you understand how these rules change, and we shall look at this later.

But mentors can also be of direct help in getting you through the glass ceiling. They can just haul you up after them. The point was made as long ago as 1978 when Hennig and Jardim wrote *The Managerial Woman*. It was based on their critical analysis of the factors which led to the success of 25 women who had reached presidential or vice-presidential levels in large companies. Amongst other things, Hennig and Jardim discovered that all these women had had mentors. And at some stage these mentors had been the immediate line managers of the women concerned, working closely with them, recognising that they could rely on their work. They had become very supportive, taking them with them to the next level, making sure they had experience in all the areas of the company that mattered. They guided them, protected them, made sure they were seen as the right people for the next job, and got them promoted. These women went through the glass ceiling as if it simply didn't exist.

They would not have been chosen as mentees, of course, had they not been competent. But they were given an extra boost by having someone powerful rooting for them.

Returning

From senior women getting towards the end of their career we turn to that very large group of women known as 'returners'. I have worked a lot with such women – town planners, secretaries, social workers, hairdressers, librarians – and my heart often bleeds at the problems they experience. They could all benefit from having mentors. Returners are, as the label suggests, women who have at some stage been in paid employment (including self-employment), but who have since then had 'time out', a period in which they have not been earning their own living. The majority of these women have had a career break in order to have and bring up their children. They are out of the workforce for a period of a few months to fifteen years or more. But there are also returners with other backgrounds, like the 'carers', single women or married, who have spent a good part of their life looking after elderly relatives. Or the wives of ex-pats, those women who have been abroad with their husbands and who have now settled to a life back in Britain and want or need to establish their own economic identity.

All these groups have their own special problems, but whether they need or want to return to work, whether they have been out for six months or several years, returners usually have a number of problems in common: they are out of touch with what goes on in today's world of work, how businesses are run, what equipment is used in offices or factories, how today's women dress for work, how women and men relate to each other as colleagues, what hierarchical structures operate, etc. They may not possess the skills needed for the jobs available to them, and may need to re-train. In most cases they have lost a good deal of confidence about their personal worth in the world beyond the home. This problem is particularly acute for women who have to go back to work because of a divorce or bereavement.

For all women, returning to work is a crucial step in their life, and networking and mentoring can ease the process considerably. Whether an individual mentor introduces them to business networks, or whether networking throws up a mentor, doesn't matter. What they need are other people, usually older women, who will help them both before they actually return to work and after they have done so.

Beforehand, mentors can encourage the women concerned to work through the organisational, training and psychological problems they will inevitably encounter, and help them to develop strategies to overcome these problems. After the women have returned to work they need a helping hand on two fronts: firstly, in juggling the needs of the workplace and the home, not forgetting the voluntary activities they used to have time for; secondly, in finding their feet in the workplace, and making up for all the lost time, so that they too have a chance to get a decent slice of the cake. They must learn as soon as possible to become colleagues rather than women returners, otherwise their prospects of promotion are nil.

So great is the importance of mentors to returners that a scheme initiated by the late Professor Daphne Jackson at the University of Surrey specifically for returning women scientists includes mentoring as an essential component. (See Chapter Seven for more details.)

Changing Career

There is yet another group of women who benefit from networking and mentoring: those who want to change career. Many of the women I have questioned for this book have done this, going from secretary to management consultant, secretary to founder manager of a printing business, clerk to post-graduate student and tutor in information technology, scientist to general manager, etc.

I myself was a case in point. After many years as a university lecturer, and enjoying it immensely, I decided that from the perspective of my life as a whole the time had come to move on. I became the Deputy General Secretary of a professional institute. I did not in fact have to learn any new skills, for I had had considerable managerial responsibility in my previous job, but the balance of skills required by the new job was very different, as was the working environment. I was greatly helped by contact with other people in similar organisations, whom I met through professional associations and the evening classes I took for company secretaries. I took these, not because I didn't have the knowledge or skill to do my new job, but because I knew I would feel more secure if I had a piece of paper that said I was competent in these things. And that was in fact of great benefit when I decided to have another change of career a few years later and started writing on career development and offering courses and private counselling. This gave me a flying start in running my own business. I had also attended a government-run scheme for people becoming self-employed, and thus expanded my network to meet people in a variety of different areas with lots of different experience from which I could benefit.

Often secretaries want to change career. By working in one section for some time they get to know the work inside out, and in many cases they are really the power behind the throne. But it is not easy to cross over. Few situations allow a secretary to step up into her boss's shoes, and I know of one firm where such a change in function is specifically forbidden. Similarly research staff in university laboratories may know all that is necessary in terms of their subject to be able to lecture in it, but changing from research to lecturing is not made easy for them.

Then there are those who want to enter completely different areas, like the social worker who wanted to become a teacher, the secretary who became an ancillary teacher in a school for handicapped children, the teacher who became a financial adviser. Whether these women stay within their original subject area or move over completely, they are all career changers, and discussing their aspirations, plans and actions with their peers in networking groups or with a mentor can spare them so many problems, and so much time.

Going Solo

There is a special group of career changers that we hear about so frequently that it merits a category of its own. This comprises the women who go solo, those who leave the corporate world and set up their own businesses. Sometimes they make their decision as a result of some specific revealing experience. They may have had a significant difference of opinion with colleagues which has made them take stock of their situation. For example, one woman thought that it was entirely misguided to cut back on the training budget; she was shocked to find that she was not only a lone voice, but out on a limb as well. So she left and set up her own training consultancy. Other women have had their heads up against the glass ceiling for a while and come to the conclusion that the best way forward for them is to get off the corporate ladder and use their talents in a way which will allow them to develop rather than stagnate, and to their own immediate benefit, rather than that of the company.

Some women stay within their own subject area, like the woman who was a senior partner in a large recruitment company, who then set up her own recruiting agency. Or they change fields completely, like the librarian who had always wanted to have a small-holding and used her redundancy money to make her dream come true. Some opt for self-employment and operate as sole traders, others establish companies and perhaps take on staff. There are yet others whose corporate experience is so useful to other companies that they make a living, often a very good one, out of picking up non-executive directorships in a range of companies.

Networking and mentoring have an extremely important part to play in the lives of women who go solo, at many different levels, before and after the move has been made. Mentors, and other network contacts, are beneficial in helping their mentees work out their real motivation. Is this a positive move, or is it made out of necessity? The truth at this stage is important in determining the kind of support a mentor needs to give her mentee. Someone who really enjoys the prospect of going solo will bring enormous enthusiasm and energy to the task, and is likely to want to talk to her mentor about the operational aspects of the new venture, who the most important contacts are, what advertising methods are most appropriate, whether equipment should be leased or purchased, etc. But someone who is haunted by her 'failure' in the corporate world, is going to require rather more psychological support, both at the time of making the move and during the later stages of the growth of the business.

Returners Going Solo

Going solo is also an option for women returners. Indeed, this may be the best option for those women who want to stay at home for whatever reason, and who also want financial independence, for they can work from home or run their business from home. They can thus fit in their domestic and work arrangements side by side. Many businesses have started from home in this way, such as chutney making, soft-toy production, secretarial services, computer program design.

Although this scheme of things has undoubted advantages for some women, it is tough. At least when working on someone else's premises you are given a structure to work in, a framework to keep you upright until you have found your feet again in the new work environment. But at home you are left to your own devices, and you have to learn to build in your own structures to keep you not only efficient but sane. Time-management is a problem. So is combatting isolation. So is making all the decisions entirely on your own. This is bad enough for a woman who has turned to self-employment after many years in structured employment, who at least knows how businesses are run. It can be even worse for a woman who may have been busy for many years, but who nevertheless did not have money-making as a primary goal. Such a woman can undoubtedly be helped by having a mentor, someone with whom to work through all the hazards and problems of self-employment and working from home, who can give psychological as well as business support, who can cajole and encourage, foresee difficulties and prevent disasters.

CHAPTER 2

Networking and Networks

I recently had a phone call out of the blue from a woman who belonged to the same professional association as I do, Women in Management (WIM). She had been asked by the chairman (male) of a very large corporation what networking was all about. She had been unable to provide a very substantial answer so, knowing from WIM that I was writing about networking and mentoring, she telephoned me to get some help. I was somewhat taken aback by this because the enquirer was a woman manager of considerable standing, so respected that she had been elected by her peers to the governing body of a major management association, up to then an all-male preserve.

I couldn't believe she didn't know what networking was. She had been doing it for years, and owed her success in large part to her ability to network. Indeed so did the chairman who had prompted the phone call. He was one of the best networkers in the business. The whole thing was on a par with a carpenter asking what a chisel was. It then dawned on me that it was precisely *because* they had been networking for years that they didn't know what it was. It was a basic tool of their trade, so much part of their daily activity that it was hardly worthy of recognition or description. The irony of the situation was that in order to find out what networking was, they were actually networking.

I gave my enquirer a few ideas on what networking was all about and how it could be helpful in career terms. I also suggested how she could set up a formal network in her organisation. I later received an invitation to the luncheon to celebrate the launch of the new network that she has now set up. As an honoured guest I was introduced to several people interested in the same things as I am. I have since met some of them again, and corresponded with others.

That is what networking is about. It means making contacts, and using those contacts for whatever purpose you need. For example, if you don't know something, ask someone else who does. Or someone who might know yet someone else who does. In the situation above, the two people concerned needed information important to them in their work, and one chat and one telephone call provided it.

Sometimes there are a few more links in the chain of communication: I recently went on a trip organised by the 300 Group (whose aim is to get more women into Parliament) to visit the Institutions of the European Community. I was on that trip because of my involvement with the Women into Public Life campaign, one of whose intentions is to get more women on to public bodies, a little understood arm of government. I met Elizabeth, who was on the trip because of her interest in getting women into Parliament. We had briefly worked together because of these similar interests. But Elizabeth is also researching therapeutic intervention in rape crisis. Knowing that most of my life has been spent in academic research, she asked me to discuss research techniques with her. Amongst other things I recommended consulting American journals to give some perspective to her British research, but was unable at that moment (we were sitting in a coach somewhere in France) to tell her where in England she could find an immediately accessible collection.

Now, Elizabeth has a daughter, who in turn has a friend called John. John is also a writer. Elizabeth, thinking he might know something about sources of American journals, spoke to him when he was visiting her house. John told her about the American Library, but wasn't sure whether it had recently moved to a new site. He thought Nanette might know. Nanette is a writing contact, a journalist. Elizabeth also knows Nanette, so she asked her about the American Library. Nanette told Elizabeth about the library in the American Embassy. Elizabeth phoned the American Embassy. They were redecorating their library so she couldn't use it, but they, belonging to the library network, told her about the United States Library housed in the Senate House library of the University of London. Elizabeth and I later met at the 300 Group Annual General Meeting and she told me all this. By the time

35

things had come full circle seven links had been involved in the chain. I don't need that information right now, but I have stored it for the time when I may need it. Or when someone else may.

The example above shows some important things about networking. The original reason for our coming together was nothing to do with rape or American journals. We had a joint interest in women and public service, and had joined the relevant groups. But through chatting at group meetings and using each other's knowledge and contacts we have established a relationship which benefits us both personally and professionally. We plugged into each other's networks, and brought the two together, forming a much bigger network. To that will be added other networks when someone else wants to know about a collection of American journals, or who is working on intervention in rape, or research techniques in general. And further note that I personally did nothing more to find out about a collection of American journals. The network developed a momentum of its own, and brought the information back to me without my steering it.

Networks then are collections of people linked by a common interest or experience, a group of contacts. And although for the purposes of this book we are interested in learning how to get career help from our networks, we must learn that the contacts who can be useful to us in this are found not only in our professional networks. We can also have useful contacts amongst our friends and neighbours. It was because my neighbour downstairs brought a woman's magazine to me when I was ill that I discovered about the fledgling Women into Public Life campaign which I now run. The important thing is to be alive to the way other people can be useful to you, in particular in job terms.

The Old Boy Network

One network which is very efficient in helping its members this way is the Old Boy Network, or OBN for short. Yes, it does exist, and its members undeniably use it to good effect. There is some dispute about the origin of the term, but it is generally believed to relate to the network of boys who were pupils at the various public schools for which Britain is famous, and which until very recently remained exclusively male territory. This was originally a small world, and remains quite small today. It is fairly easy, as a result, for the old boys of these schools to keep in touch, especially since their fathers have probably been to the same public schools, so there is already a family connection linking the pupils. The old boys have a very efficient grapevine and look after their own. If something good is in the offing word gets round very fast. And the goodies (including jobs) get distributed to those inside the network, and not outside it.

Whether they *actively* seek to keep others out from influential positions is a moot point, but they do seem rather to hog the scene. Tim Heald's book on this; *Networks: Who We Know and How We Use Them*, is very revealing. He expands the meaning of OBN to include men who were together at the same university, or indeed university college, for he feels that very strong links of loyalty and mutual trust are formed during that time, as they are during service in the same regiment. He documents beautifully that what we call 'The Establishment' is fairly well populated by the OBN. We are talking about senior members of the Church (in particular the Anglican Church, the 'established' Church of England), the Army, the Civil Service, the Law, and the City, as well as the worlds of medicine and learning. The OBN also operates in government bodies of all kinds, whether the individuals are 'elected' openly, or 'appointed' in a rather more obscure procedure. Members of the OBN are now to be found at the top of manufacturing industry too, though this is a fairly recent development (see Müller-Mees on male networks in Germany).

Nowadays, of course, the OBN, as a network, extends far beyond former pupils of public schools. Men have recognised the importance of the system and have learned to emulate the networking skills of the original members, so any effective male network now tends to be called an old boy network, no matter how tenuous its historical link to public schools. Indeed newcomers can emulate the originals so successfully that they are virtually indistinguishable from them. Heald calls them the 'establishmentarians', as distinct from the original 'foundationers'.

Through their occupancy of top jobs the OBN enables its members to achieve and maintain power and money, and to keep them in the trusted hands of those who share common values. But women can't join the OBN. The OBN accepts only those in its own image, and women are not propagated in the image of men. Even those women who have attended formerly all male public schools are hardly considered part of the OBN. But we can learn from the networking system that the OBN uses. Having seen some of the benefits, we can learn in detail how it works and we can adapt it to our own requirements. We won't follow it wholesale, of course, for a wholly male system will not wholly suit women, but we will take what we need and use it to get our slice of the pie.

Women Networking

Lest you should feel daunted at the prospect of emulating, or at least emulating the best parts of, the OBN, let me reassure you: we women have a flying start. Women have been networking for years, but we haven't called it that. We have called it 'caring', for that is how we have traditionally used our networks: to take care of the needs of other people.

Women are naturally good at networking. When contact is made between new neighbours it is most often the wives who establish contact first, offering tea and biscuits during the actual moving in, and advice on local facilities shortly thereafter: the best shops, the best schools, the doctors, restaurants, etc. Women have a whole network of contacts that they welcome other women into, so that they can manage their 'business', their domestic business, efficiently. Strange then, that we stand in awe of the efficacy of the old boy network, when so much vital networking is done by women. This distorted view of our own abilities is again due to the different socialisation of men and women that we mentioned earlier. The management of the family, the domestic business of many women, is not paid, does not contribute in a direct or officially acknowledged way to the economic well-being of the country. It is therefore discounted in public (male and female) eyes. The very same networking skills that develop a man's career are undervalued and devalued when they are exercised by women in the pursuit of household and family management. Men network. But women gossip.

But of course women can and do use networks to further a career of paid work. They have been doing it for years to support the careers of their husbands.

Let us look at a small example. One male departmental head

says to another male departmental head: 'My wife was wondering whether you and your wife would like to come to dinner next week. Nothing grand, just the four of us.' Second head replies: 'Well, that's very nice of you. Let me just make a note of the date, and I'll ask my wife. She looks after the social side of things.'

That is what men call women's ability to keep life going. To keep the wheels (even of professional organisations) oiled. The social side of things brings people together as human beings rather than holders of posts, allowing them to *express* (I use the word advisedly) aspects of themselves not normally welcome in organisational life, like *feeling* it's all a bit much sometimes, and just wishing Humphries would occasionally shut up at meetings. But then the colleague (after three glasses of wine, perhaps he is really a *friend*?) replies that we won't have to put up with old Humphries much longer anyway, he's on his way out. Or so the rumour goes. Good source, though. The usual channels. Going to be replaced by that Scottish chap, the one who did so well in that outward-bound course. Good course, that. Chairman's very impressed. Thought we might give it a go.

Let's examine what is going on here. At a dinner party two male colleagues are chatting about an interest they have in common: work. Ostensibly they are talking about an irritating colleague likely soon to be replaced by a Scot who is good at outdoor pursuits. But that is only the official agenda. There is also a hidden agenda to which they can address themselves, thanks to the safe, protected environment of the dinner party. Without ever being explicit they are re-affirming a bond of mutual allegiance. They exchange secrets, information which they have heard on the grapevine; admit to a weakness, the human frailty of frustration; discuss the background and abilities of the new colleague so that they have at least two areas of small talk with which to ingratiate themselves. (Sorry – to welcome him, to let him know he is among friends.) Also by sharing information about the chairman's latest whim, the outward-bound course, they are protecting each other from his possible displeasure, and offering each other future mutual support by going on the outward-bound course together. And an additional benefit would be that it might lead to their promotion too, a benefit for at least one of them, which would also benefit the other, in reward for his continuing loyalty.

This is allegiance building and maintenance. It is an example of organisational politics. Each man and each woman knew when the invitation was offered and accepted that the dinner party would be a euphemism for a private meeting to thrash out the tactics of coping with the new arrival and the chairman's preferences. The wives, of course, take no part in the actual words of the discussion, but it is they who stage-manage the whole thing. It is they who have listened to their husbands at home, they who have decided that the moment has come for some private networking, they who have networked to get the idea of the dinner party off the ground, and they who have done the actual work so that their husbands could network informally for the preservation of their own power.

This reveals a major difference in the purpose to which men and women traditionally put their networking skills. Men network for their own power. But women, whether they tell other women about the best shops, or arrange dinner parties for their husband, network to support other people, and the power of other people. They have even in the past established their own formal networks to do this, what have been traditionally called 'women's organisations'. These often focus on issues which enable women better to serve their family and their community. The TG, for example, the Townswomen's Guild, is amongst the better known. It was established 'to advance the education of women irrespective of race, creed and party so as to enable them to make the best contribution to the common good' (WNC directory). And most of the charitable organisations of this country would never have seen the light of day if it had not been for the unpaid work of women of all classes.

This means that women have a long history of networking. So what we have to learn from the OBN is to support our own career, not only to service the needs of others. Fortunately more and more women are learning to use networking skills in pursuit of their own power. Though this appears not to be general knowledge. An article in the *Guardian* as recent as May 1990, asserts that women use school networks just to keep up with friends. But we do use network contacts for work purposes. I empathise with the comments attributed to the woman Member of Parliament, Emma Nicholson, about old school networks: 'I am very pleased now when someone makes contact; my last researcher came to me because his mother was at school with my eldest sister.' And with

Drusilla Beyfus who summed it up: 'The only real network is that of women who work.'

We should pause at this point to note that what we have been talking about so far relates to networking as a way of behaving, and the networks we have mentioned (except the TG) have been loosely constructed groups of people who know each other because of common interests or experiences. Although the OBN is referred to as a network, it too is an informal grouping.

Having seen what networking can do for men's career development, we women have become more aware of the networking opportunities we have in our lives. But we have decided to go one step further and create networking groups of our own, with the specific intention that they should be useful to us in career terms. It was only to be expected that they would be labelled in line with men's networks. So we now have the NGNs, the new girl networks.

New Girl Networks

This term refers to those networking groups which have been established in the last twenty years or so, to meet the needs of the increasing number of women in paid employment. Women in Management (WIM) led the field in 1969, followed by City Women's Network in 1978, and Network in 1981. These are open to women from a range of work areas, but all have the promotion of women to senior management positions as a fundamental concern. But from the late seventies date other organisations like Women in Publishing (1979), Women in Banking (1980), Women in Medicine (1981), Women in Housing (1981), Women Architects Group (1985), Women in Dentistry (1985), Women in Fundraising Development (1987), Women in Computing (1988), Women in Higher Education Network (1989), etc. They exist to ensure that women are treated equally with men in training and employment in specific work areas.

The Women Returners' Network also caters for a specific group, not this time determined by subject, but by their desire to get back into the workforce after a career break to look after children or relatives. This was created in 1984. And since 1989 we have had an umbrella organisation, the National Alliance of Women's Organisations (NAWO), which promotes the charitable aims common to or supported by the 176 women's organisations which are affiliated to it. Many of these relate to women's paid employment.

Some women's professional networking groups, however, have a much longer history. The Women's Engineering Society, for example, was founded in 1919, and the Association of Women Solicitors (the 1919 Club) in 1923, the latter name reflecting the general if reluctant opening up of the professions to women with the passing of the Sex Discrimination (Removal) Act in 1919.

Women's groups operate differently according to their members' interests. Some allow anyone (including men) who supports their stated aims to become members, eg. Women in Management. Others restrict membership to those in certain categories. These can be defined by subject (Women in Banking, see Balsdon), or by employment in a particular company, like Women in BP (see Jackson). Others cater for women in one area at certain levels of seniority, as in the European Association of Professional Secretaries.

This last one also demonstrates another new phenomenon amongst women's organisations – the European connection. We now have, for example, the European Women's Management Development Network, and NAWO has recently established a European Women's Lobby.

There are also women's sections of professional groups, like the Institute of Physics, or the London Chamber of Commerce. The women who belong to these are members of the main group, but have set up the special interest group to address specific problems.

Most of these networking groups have a formal structure, with a constitution setting out their aims and the rules by which they shall be governed. They have an elected governing body. They are usually subscription organisations, with an annual membership fee. Some are federal organisations with more or less autonomy exercised in the various regional groups. Some are big enough to have salaried staff, in addition to honorary officers. Many of them lobby government and others on behalf of members. Most of them publish a newletter, and several issue a directory of members. Most of them arrange a programme of seminars or other events. Whilst most of these events are work-orientated, there are always times before and after the set piece which allow informal meeting, 'networking', between members. Some organisations hold specific 'networking meetings'.

Indeed the primary function of several women's groups is to allow members to network amongst each other. There are for example the various dining clubs, some with private membership. A fairly recent arrival on the English scene is a breakfast club, the Belgravia Breakfast Club, the brainchild of Sandra Hepburn from Thames Television. As a senior executive she had few female peers, and felt the need to meet and share experiences with other women in a similar position. At this time Doreen Boulding was general manager of the Belgravia-Sheraton Hotel and she became a co-founder of the Club, offering the hotel as a meeting place. Since senior women are very busy people the best time they thought people could get together was before work, so the meetings take place at 7.45 am on the last Thursday of the month. Since then Doreen has moved on, and the meetings are now held at the Sheraton Park Tower. The hotel offers the coffee or orange juice as its contribution to women's development. There is no subscription, but each woman attending contributes a minimum of £10 which is accumulated for a year and then sent to a women's health charity. There are no set events, only occasionally a few announcements. A list of regular participants is produced for networking purposes, but nothing more. The sole purpose is to let women meet and share common concerns and information in a relaxed social setting, while simultaneously supporting a charity. Doreen's move to The Old Swan at Harrogate has resulted in the founding of the first regional branch in the north-east. It is hoped to establish a Scottish branch in Edinburgh towards the end of 1991. Forum UK is another group for senior women which networks over breakfast. Chaired by Jean Denton CBE, it is a partner in the International Women's Forum, and enables members to network worldwide.

Networking possibilities are also provided by magazines like *Cosmopolitan* and *Good Housekeeping* who run occasional work-related courses. This allows women of like interest to get to know each other and remain in touch, perhaps going on several courses together. And the Pepperell Unit of the Industrial Society also holds Saturday workshops for women, which perform the same function.

The new networking groups are not clubs with their own premises, like the famous gentlemen's clubs. There are such clubs for women, like the University Women's Club, and they can be used for professional networking purposes. But they were not set up specifically to do that, and provide a range of membership services beyond what we have been talking about. The usual thing is for a new networking group to hire club or hotel premises for its meetings, and perhaps negotiate cheap rates for the use of specific facilities like the gym or sauna.

The social function of all these networks is very attractive and important, and roundly refutes an extraordinary statement made in Tim Heald's otherwise perceptive book on networks. He says '. . . men genuinely enjoy the company of other men, whereas women on the whole don't much enjoy the exclusive company of women' (p178). Where he gets his information from I cannot think. Certainly not from the women I am in regular contact with, whether they belong to the newer or the older women's groups. The Fawcett Society has been going since 1866, the National Federation of Women's Institutes since 1915, the TG since 1929, and the United Kingdom Federation of Business and Professional Women since 1938. They could not have survived if women networking with women were not an enjoyable as well as a professionally useful experience.

Networking with other women is often very exhilarating. Women show immense good will to each other, and share their knowledge and experience with great generosity. And this also happens across national boundaries. Women travelling around the world need only let an appropriate women's network in the destination countries know, and offers of accommodation and hospitality will arise spontaneously.

The Basic Benefits of Networking

Having made the distinction between networks and networking, let us look at some of the basic benefits that active networking can bring, whether we are talking about networking in women's groups or not. We are, of course, interested in benefits which will allow us to develop our career. We want to become more informed and more competent as employees, colleagues, bosses, with appropriate promotion, authority, etc. But we also want to become better people, both in a job context and beyond. This distinction corresponds roughly to what Kram has labelled career benefits on the one hand, and psychosocial benefits on the other (see Kram, *Mentoring at Work*). We shall start by looking at an obvious career benefit, that of finding a new job.

Jobs

'Being there at the right time' can be crucial in finding work. Many jobs worth having are not advertised, so it is important to belong to networks where members can give you information about vacancies. Indeed a lot of 'headhunting' takes place in women's organisations. Women who work in executive search are forever looking out for new people whom they can pass on to their client organisations.

But you don't have to be a headhunter to be able to refer people. I was recently giving private counselling to a woman returner. She was going through a messy divorce, had very little money, had left serious work behind long before, had virtually no self-confidence left, but now needed work desperately. I was helping her to put together a cv which would reveal what she was capable of. She had an enormous range of skills learned in a variety of part-time jobs and voluntary work. I was convinced she was someone who would make a success of her return to work given half a chance, and indeed saw her grow visibly in confidence as we went through the list of things in which she had demonstrated competence.

On this particular day it was convenient to meet in a spare office in a friend's organisation, the friend who had put us in touch. The friend and I knew each other through women's employment networks. Suddenly the door opened and in walked someone who had come to see the friend whose office we were using. But we also knew each other quite well, from another network. She, not realising I was in private session, chatted briefly, told me about her new job and said that she was looking for staff to do a range of administrative jobs. If I knew anyone, I was to let her know. By the end of that afternoon my client and I had put together a promising cv. I sent her off to contact the person who had just breezed through the office. To cut a long story short, she applied for one of the vacant positions. She did not get the job. But on the spot she was offered another position in the same company which suited her skills better! I have seen her several times since, and the transformation is wonderful. She is now actively preparing for the next job, and has joined crucial networks.

Networking works. Figures vary, but it is undeniable that a good many jobs are filled without public advertisement, and 'contacts in the right places' are vital. If a woman applies before the job is generally advertised, she lets it be known that she has the right contacts. She will, in a sense, already have passed muster before she is told of the job, so she is at least guaranteed a reasonable hearing by the selectors. Also, by applying early, or at least asking for information and thereby letting it be known that she could be available if the conditions were right, she demonstrates initiative, autonomy, and ambition. And these are all important features to demonstrate, along with the appropriate job skills.

Self-employed women have constantly to find new jobs, so their networks are a life-support system. It is vital for them to build up a large network of contacts to let people know what their product is and how good it is, and to locate their target market. An investigation by Carter and Cannon commissioned by the Department of Employment and Shell UK into female entrepreneurship recommends that

> Female entrepreneurs experiencing problems of credibility should be encouraged by their advisers to use a strategy of persistent and planned networking to achieve a positive outcome (p21).

Recommendations

With a good network around you you do not even have to 'be there' to get a job. Your contacts can recommend you. A fellow member from Women in Management phoned me to say that she had been asked to recommend some women who would be suitable to serve on the council of an education college in London. She phoned me, not because she wanted to put me forward at that time (I didn't have the right qualifications) but because she knew that I have a very wide contact base. My contact wanted access to my contacts. I was able to supply her with four suitable names, and she passed the message on to the director of the college in question. He has since been in direct touch with me about the women concerned, for he was interested in all of them. But he would not have known about me had it not been for our intermediary contact. That director is now in my database of contacts and I in his, and we have been in touch since on different matters of importance to us both.

And while I was writing this chapter I was asked to put someone forward as a non-executive director of a public body. I found that the criteria matched a WIM network contact, a founder director of a public limited company. I phoned her to ask if she were interested. At this moment she has other plans which might conflict, so she declined, but she mentioned a colleague in her own company who might be suitable. She said: 'You know X, don't you? You've talked to her. You know what calibre of person she is. Have you thought of putting her forward?' I hadn't. But I have now.

Information Resource

All kinds of job-related knowledge and information can be gathered at network meetings if you keep your ears open. You can learn not just about sources of American journals, but the latest photocopying equipment, imminent redundancy in such and such a company, who is thinking of moving on, etc. This is an invaluable benefit of networking, for it speeds up the process of getting vital information, sparing you personally the need to go through all the business and trade papers, and personally to attend all the conferences. And whilst many women's networks issue a newsletter full of information, there is no substitute for being in a meeting yourself, actively contributing to the circulation of relevant information, asking for details and following appropriate information up before everyone else gets there.

The Specific Benefits of Networking with Women

There are additional career and psychosocial benefits which we can acquire if we belong to a women's group specifically set up to help women gain whatever knowledge, skills, experience and practice they need to grow as people and employees. But let us not forget that many of these benefits can also be derived from general networking amongst women.

Non-Male Environment

The advantage offered by a non-male environment should not be discounted. A situation in which the traditional female values of support and cooperation rule the day is such a relief after battling

47

against unadulterated male, if not macho, values all week. Many women are able to learn better in all-female groups, and this is important to career development.

And some women find it easier to relax when there are no men around, being on edge and apprehensive in the company of male colleagues, not knowing quite what to expect. (The reverse, of course, is also true. Some men are uncomfortable in the presence of female colleagues. Even hardened male trade unionists, quite capable of facing a hostile male audience, have been known to turn tail in front of a 'horde of screaming women'. And I have seen a Minister for Employment literally run out of a room when he had finished reading his prepared speech to an audience of women trainers!)

Relaxation

Relaxation is important to growing, and women's groups provide a bolt-hole, a safe-house, a non-tense environment in which to relax, have a drink, a chat, and just exist without constant challenge, either from the job or colleagues. Just being in a de-stressing environment is enormously helpful in getting your job, your career, or simply the problems of the day, in perspective. It also allows you to recharge your batteries. It is true that you can get some of these things in your own home, but there you rarely meet other professionals with whom to discuss things, and you usually have other pressing responsibilities. Better to get away from it all.

We all enjoy the company of people of like mind. But there are relatively few women in work situations, especially in management positions, so women have difficulty in finding women of like mind in the workplace. And the few women you meet there may not be the sort with whom you would want to have closer contact. You don't have to like your colleagues just because they are women. A network provides you with a choice of women with whom to relax and socialise.

Women now assert without embarrassment that some of their needs are best met in an all-female group. But I am not for one second proposing that women separate for ever from the company of men. What I am saying is that single-sex groups have legitimate functions in our society. Helping women to develop in career terms is one of them.

There is nothing new in single-sex clubs where the members relax and draw breath. The gentleman's clubs of London and other major cities in Britain have been providing this benefit to their members for years. What is wrong with them is not that they are single-sex, but that they are very important places for getting business and career information, and if women are excluded from the clubs, they are excluded from vital business networks and are thus at an unfair disadvantage.

Doing Business

Most gentleman's clubs frown on doing business at the club, but it is amazing how many deals just magically materialise over a glass of brandy. Women's networks do not forbid business. Quite the opposite. In great measure they have been set up specifically to provide business contacts and to deal with business topics. They deliberately give members the chance to make contacts which are useful to them in their career. I have been at many all-women meetings where members arrange to do business with each other, like someone needing printing giving the contract to a printer who is a network member. Or someone else moving her business account because she can get better service at a bank where a member works.

Role Models

Women are enormously helped by meeting at close quarters women who have 'made it', and this is a very important benefit of networking. It is of particular significance for younger women who do not have any successful women in their own working environments. These women are living proof that women can be successful. They supply the evidence that much of the early experience of young girls fails to provide, of successful career women as well as career men. The benefit to the younger members of the network is that they can mix with these successful beings and relate to them as women. They can thus emotionally feel rather than just intellectually know that success for women is within the realms of the possible. They can learn of their route to success, their pitfalls and their turning points, see how they conduct themselves, how they speak, relate to other people, etc. They can begin to see the parallels between their own life and that of the successful women, identifying with them in a very true sense and, inspired by them,

49

begin to model themselves on them, consciously or unconsciously.

There is no doubt that prestigious and successful women set the tone of the network they belong to. Not only do they serve as direct role models for some women, but they inspire success in all other members. Successful women are therefore very much in demand in their networks. Pearl Shaw is one such woman. She is the world-wide doyenne of networking among women in the travel business. As she put it to me: 'I find that I am constantly on call to assist younger women seeking promotion or new jobs and giving them names of contacts, advice and information.'

Expectation of Success

But rubbing shoulders with successful women also has a more intangible benefit. You are touched by their glory, and this touch stays with you. A feeling develops of being at home with success, that success is right and comfortable. And the power of this sensation cannot be underestimated. Anything other than success is unthinkable. So every member of that network knows that her pathway leads up. You belong, therefore you will succeed. How can it be otherwise?

The expectation of success is a very important benefit of belonging to a network, and has been proved time and again. Boys who go to Eton expect to become leaders. And they do.

Training

Many women's networks run their own training courses. On these all-female courses women can learn and practise skills. For example, women traditionally fail to demonstrate leadership skills in a mixed group discussion. This is something they must urgently correct, for leadership qualities vital to advancement are often revealed (and spotted by a superior) in group discussion – opening negotiations, encouraging others to participate, offering opinions without waiting to be asked, summarising discussions, cutting through unnecessary rhetoric, etc. Research reported by Sargent (p61) and others show that women learn to perform such skills, and then learn to perform them better in mixed groups after they have had a chance to practise in all-female groups. In my own courses I have heard women say what a relief it is to be able to make mistakes (and learn from them) without their male colleagues there to gloat at the slightest error.

There are several skills areas typically treated by women's networks. Presentation skills, for example, so that you are properly trained to make a good impression for your proposals. Financial sophistication too is fundamental to business, but it is a skill which few women have been encouraged to develop. Computer literacy is also vital, and is another area where women need to catch up, for computing has often been taught on the back of mathematics, an area in which girls have not been adequately encouraged. Indeed, many courses run by women's networks are compensatory, taught specifically to help women catch up in areas where men have a cultural lead, so that they can then compete in a mixed gender workplace on a more equal footing.

A side benefit of courses arranged by women's groups is that they are usually run by women trainers, offering the trainees role models of competent women, to balance the number of male trainers with whom they are confronted.

In addition to teaching *specific* skills, women's networks can also provide training in things like yoga or meditation, for women are often more prepared than men to consider 'alternative' techniques of handling problems. They are more likely than men, for example, to question whether high levels of stress are really necessary. Indeed they often believe that a high level of stress is actually counterproductive in getting the job done, and they actively seek to reduce their stress levels. This they can do in professional networks, retaining all the benefits of professional networking, yet being protected from the scornful comments of (male) colleagues who have not yet travelled the same distance down the spiritual path.

Extra Expertise and Visibility

By taking active part in the activities of a women's network you can develop a range of skills and knowledge which your present job does not call for or allow you to learn. For example, some women's networks have a lobbying function. They put forward to government or other authoritative bodies their collective views on training, employment law, child-care facilities, pension rights, etc, thus making the voice of their members heard more effectively than if they were to approach such authorities individually. By contributing to the debate on such matters, undertaking the research or helping with the presentation, generally taking a

51

responsible part in a team effort, you are making yourself more flexible in employment terms, giving yourself the edge over someone with your company experience, but not your network experience. For example, you may want to apply for a project manager's position. This will require team-working skills, some knowledge of employment law, presentation skills, etc. all of which you have learned in your network, not in your job, but which you can refer to in your application.

Such activity also gives you public visibility and draws the attention of your current employers and potential future ones to your competence and ability to take the broader view. The 'broader view' is absolutely indispensable to advancement, and women must learn to take it and be seen to be taking it.

But active membership of a women's network is not just a rehearsal for the man's world. Women are in business too, as owners, directors, senior managers, and they can offer you a job or recommend you elsewhere. The more you are seen to be competent and good to work with, the greater your chances of being known generally as someone worth watching and worth promoting.

Support and Alliance Building

The workplace can be a very frustrating place for women. Male values reign supreme, not because male values are necessarily the best for the workplace, but because traditionally the workplace has been populated with men with male values. Many of the skills that are normal in the workplace are not taught to women, therefore women have little opportunity to learn or practise them beforehand. And when they do enter the workplace they are confronted with the need to demonstrate skills that they haven't had a chance to learn. They therefore feel threatened by their own apparent incompetence. This is particularly disorientating when they know they have high levels of technical skills, but they lack (apparently) a whole slew of other skills nobody told them about. And they only know of them because men are getting the promotions and they are not.

The following quotation from Sargent describes a situation in which many women have found themselves:

If she has trouble adjusting, all too often the system conveys to the

52

confused woman the message that there is something wrong with her. This message is easily believed. As a result, she views the problem as hers, and her solution is to try to change herself. The system is not questioned. In this way, the woman chooses to be the victim of the situation rather than challenging the system's values (p147).

Belonging to a woman's network can help a lone woman deal with this problem positively. Firstly, it can reassure her that the problem is not specific to her. Secondly, 'a problem shared is a problem halved': the company of others gives us perspective on our situation and allows us to look at it more dispassionately. Our female training in humility teaches us to see the problem as ours, but when we get together and see that we are all experiencing the same thing, we realise that it is unlikely for 52 per cent of the population all to be wrong. Thirdly, the woman concerned can go through this situation together with the others and see if their combined experience can find a way to improve things for her.

An example of such a problem is finding that men in a committee often cut into what a woman is saying, or ignore her point and make it themselves, being congratulated for their perspicacity while the woman is left in bewildered isolation. In a women's network she can learn that this is a problem frequently encountered by single women on committees. She can also practise with other members techniques for getting her point across, using her own values, as well as the male values of her colleagues.

There are also times when a woman needs urgent and supportive help from her networks, and needs to gather allies about her. For example, a short while ago a lone female colleague was treated shabbily by her affiliates. She turned to her network for help. As a consequence two members of her network, each with complementary knowledge of employment and contract law, are helping her to bring a case for breach of contract. Going to law is always stressful, but she is finding strength in their united stand against the foe.

Active Networking

Just being in a network is not enough. Networking is active, dynamic. To use your networks fully you have to be 'go-getting'.

This is something of a problem for British women, who are under a strong cultural restraint not to say what they want; they have been brought up not to be 'pushy'. It is still pretty difficult for some women even to introduce themselves to people they don't know, let alone ask them for help. But the situation is different on the other side of the Atlantic. When Irma Kurtz (an American) launched Jane Grant's book *Sisters across the Atlantic: Networking in the USA* at the American Embassy, she said soberly that in Britain women wanted a fair slice of the cake; and then proclaimed triumphantly that in America they wanted 'the whole gorgeous hunk!' And Mary Scott Welch gives some splendid examples of how American women do things, including networking in the ladies' loo. At a networking lunch in San Francisco, sponsored by the Professional Women's Alliance, Roxanne Mankin, who owns a specialist real estate company, is in one cubicle, talking to the woman in the next. She says that she is looking for a new comptroller for her company. Suddenly an excited voice yells from a third cubicle:

'I'll be right out!' So there, in the perfect locker room atmosphere of the old boys' network, Joan Mills, an executive searcher specialising in women in the financial area, finds a new client in Roxanne (p56).

Perhaps this is still a little advanced for the non-American woman. But networking is a career tool not to be ignored. It is powerful enough for women to make the effort to overcome their cultural barriers.

- You must develop and use your contacts.
- You must try to get along to meetings, even if the topic is not of direct relevance to you, to meet other people.
- Make sure you *always* have a supply of business cards to distribute at meetings, or to send to people from whom you extract cards, possibly with a cv to show your own interests.
- Send cards at Christmas or New Year to remind your new contacts that you exist.
- Ask around to find out who has the information and influence that you need.
- At all times keep your eyes and ears open for anything that is useful, follow it up and use it, or store the information away for future use.

But networking is two-sided, and the second side is second nature to British women: active networking also means being useful yourself, lending a copy of a report, for example, or offering information and advice, passing on tips and anecdotes, contributing to a newsletter. You may then, quite legitimately even in British terms, expect to receive similar support yourself, not necessarily on the same day, or from the same people, but via the sort of network chain that we looked at earlier in this chapter.

There are plenty of networks of which you might be part: professional societies, trade associations, trade unions, chambers of commerce, local business groups. All these can help you in your career. It is up to you to see that they do.

And don't forget that skills and visibility can cross borders. Try running for office in your various networks to gain a range of skills which you can then use to gain promotion in your employment. This applies not only to professional networks, but also sports clubs, and informal groups. If you are the treasurer of an organisation you are demonstrating the trust of your fellow citizens in both your integrity and your financial ability. Or you may be active in a local charity or other voluntary public service, like being a school governor, which would give you further credibility at work. The duties of school governors nowadays are quite considerable, and being a governor will increase the range of responsibilities, skills and experience, (legal, financial, personnel management), which you can rely on when applying for promotion.

But the really important thing is not just to do it, but to let it be known that you do it. Make sure knowledge about yourself is transferred from network to network, to increase the number of people who know about your competence, to help you get where you want to go.

The Wrong Networks

Throughout this chapter networking has been seen as a positive thing, giving you ever-increasing access to powerful people who can influence your development and promotion. But a word of caution must be added about 'negative' networks. You may, without knowing it, be 'symbolised' as belonging to a particular network, when you are not in fact a member. For members of networks, like members of clubs, often have some identifying feature or symbol about them, like the old school tie, and the sporting of this symbol, even unwittingly, will indicate membership of the wrong networks and tell against you.

Dress and accent are potent symbols. I once had the difficult task of explaining to a Conservative lady that she had little chance of being selected as a parliamentary candidate in her chosen area because of her excessively plummy voice. No one would have believed that she, with a voice and accent like that, could conceivably have had any empathy with people other than the very privileged. Shortly after that I had to tell a Labour lady that wearing trousers to her selection meeting wasn't going to do her much good. It may have been a socialist borough, but they wanted a candidate who knew how to dress on formal occasions. Both of them protested to me that they didn't conform to the images that their symbols were implying. That didn't matter. What mattered was that the selection panel believed they belonged to networks that didn't belong in their neck of the woods, and they weren't selected.

Networking and Career Success

But to my mind the greatest career benefits are *learning* to network and becoming *sensitised* to the very existence, system and influence of informal networks. The importance of the organisational network, the informal system to which men belong and women are excluded, because of their history and socialisation, is emphasised by Hennig and Jardim throughout their excellent book, *The Managerial Woman*. If there is one single message that comes across from this book it is that if women want to climb the corporate ladder they must learn about the informal system and must learn to use it as effectively as the men do.

They alert women to the dangers of relying on formal structures and policies, rather than seeking out and becoming part of the influential informal networks. They suggest that women believe that if they teach themselves to jump through the hoops placed at critical points in their careers they will progress:

[Women emphasise] individual self-improvement as the critical factor determining career advancement. This in itself is related to the sense of passivity, to the overwhelming sense of 'waiting to be chosen'. It depends for its rationale upon a belief in the effectiveness of the formal structure, formal definitions, roles, policies, the way things should be, and what it critically omits is a sense of the organisational environment – the informal system of relationships and information sharing, ties of loyalty and of dependence, of favors granted and owed, of mutual benefit, of protection – which men unfailingly and invariably take into account to however greater or lesser a degree (p12).

Their message applies to all women who want a career rather than just a job. And it applies in greater measure the further up the career ladder you go. They are referring to the American scene. The same applies in Britain. Tim Heald, a self-confessed member of the British old boy network, puts it this way:

They [the people responsible for senior appointments] will deal with others, of course, politely perhaps, but without the real sense of enthusiasm reserved for fellow members of their various networks – the people who together comprise their PPN (Private Personal Network) (p241).

Substitute 'women' for 'others' and you will see what we are up against.

Networking and Mentors

Many important aspects of networking can be learned by a woman trying to climb up the career ladder alone. But to get beyond the glass ceiling she must gain access to the most influential networks, learn how they work and be able to compete against the men (and the few women) who are already there. The best way for you to do this is to be introduced and guided by someone who already belongs and who thinks that you are worth the investment of time and attention. This means looking for a mentor, for this is the sort of benefit that your mentor can provide. Mentors can teach you to network. And mentors can also be found by networking. The two are intimately linked.

57

Emma Nicholson MP

Emma Nicholson is an extraordinary woman in a number of ways. She is a leading member of many different networks and through her achievements in her personal and professional life acts as a role model for other women. She is a computer specialist, but is particularly concerned about the possible misuse of computers and information technology. She is also a musician by training, and combines this with her interest in the disabled by chairing 'Access for Disabled People to Arts Premises Today'. Her work for children's welfare includes a period as Director of Fundraising for the 'Save the Children Fund', an interest which she is still pursuing actively by her fact-finding visits to the children in Romanian orphanages. She is also a Trustee of the Suzy Lamplugh Trust, an organisation which helps women in particular to improve their personal safety, and of forty-odd other charities.

In addition to all this, Emma Nicholson is a politician of considerable renown: she was Vice-Chairman of the Conservative Party from 1983 to 1987, and has been MP for Torridge and West Devon since 1987.

Emma Nicholson has thus sought and accepted high public office. In meeting the responsibilities of such roles she lays great stress on the importance of personal integrity. She is supported in this by her deeply held Christian faith.

But she also gratefully acknowledges the help of the mentors who have guided her on her way. She believes that that it is crucial for all of us to have people to admire in our working as well as our private lives, and recognises Michael Alison MP and Bernard Weatherill MP, the Speaker of the House of Commons, as her role models. Both are committed to truth, and have the highest integrity. They are rigorous in their political thinking, and are exceptionally hard and consistent workers. And both show personal humility. These are qualities that she admires and has tried to emulate in her work in Parliament and beyond.

Emma Nicholson's achievements are all the greater for the courage and perseverance they require, for she was born profoundly deaf. She is therefore herself a role model and very public inspiration to all those struggling against difficulty to achieve their personal goals, in whatever area of life they choose. Her hearing is wholly corrected now by modern science and she works to get these benefits widely available to all.

CHAPTER 3

Finding and Using a Mentor

The last chapter discussed the considerable benefits that active networking brings to someone wanting to develop her career. In networking everyone contributes to a pool of knowledge and experience and everyone takes from it. Mentoring provides you with many of the same benefits, but there is an important added benefit of having a one-to-one relationship: you will be the focus of attention of one particular person who thinks you are worth spending time and effort on. She will have recognised in you a talent and a potential, and will want to help you realise them to the full. She will be someone who has already made a success of her career, knows how to get up the ladder, and wants to haul you up behind her.

The power of such attention specifically given to you should not be underestimated. Depending on whether you and she work in the same company, the same field of work, or entirely different areas, she will provide you with a range of benefits: she will help, guide and advise you, open doors for you, protect you when you are weak, give you your head when you are strong.

But she can't do this unless she knows you exist and that you have a capacity and desire for development. Many a flower has blossomed unseen and wasted its scent on the desert air because nobody happened to be passing at the time. Instead of getting themselves about a bit, these flowers 'waited' to be appreciated, in the traditional innocent female belief that goodness is bound to be rewarded. Women often go to their graves still waiting: waiting to be asked for their hand in marriage, waiting to be asked to join a committee, waiting to be promoted. Waiting for the prince to come along and discover them in the glass coffin, under the glass ceiling, to bend low over them, and with a kiss awaken them to be the next chairperson of ICI. Sir John Harvey-Jones's book is called, with reason, *Making It Happen*. Women should learn to do the same.

Women might have sufficient wit to see an opportunity when it comes along, and they might have sufficient energy to turn the opportunity to good advantage, but what about all the other opportunities they could have turned to even greater advantage if they had created the opportunities in the first place?

One of my own mentees was a classic case. She didn't find or even look for me, but when a friend told her that she might find me helpful as a mentor she seized the opportunity. A year earlier she had left a comfortable but non-challenging job because of family circumstances. She had had a short fixed-term assignment with a small organisation, but that had come to an end and she was now looking for permanent employment. She told me vehemently that she wanted to work for a large organisation with lots of different departments. She demonstrated real aggression as she said this, a feature I had not previously seen in her. She went on to explain that she was sick of using only half her talents, so she wanted to work for an organisation where they had a need for a range of talents, and where they would (presumably) assess her and move her around to where her skills could be put to best use.

She was, of course, waiting for other people to spot her and develop her, and her aggression was born of frustration because people hadn't in the main been doing this. I saw part of my job with her as converting this aggession into action, pro-active action, so that she would go out and get things for herself.

She has surpassed all expectations. From being a pleasant but not very exciting person, she has blossomed into a go-getter, mapping out the future ahead of her. After putting considerable effort into her cv and her interviewing skills she found a job. It is a job which does not and cannot in its present form use all of her talents, but she is using it as a learning experience and as a stepping stone to the next stage up. She keeps a regular note of things she has done and what she has learned, enjoyed or disliked. She has joined a women's professional organisation and goes regularly to their meetings; has also joined a non-professional group; has had herself assessed with psychometric tests to help her plan her next career move; has developed a better relationship with her family, and generally looks much better and healthier, and is a joy to be with. She has also just had a substantial salary increase. She is a radically different person for channelling her energy into planning rather than letting it wither on the vine while she waited to be spotted. She comes back to me for occasional reassurance, to get my reaction to her next move, but she doesn't really need me any more. She has definitely become her own person.

Exactly the same thing applies to finding a mentor. Don't passively wait for one to come along. Be active. Take your development into your own hands. Think about what it is you want from a mentor, then find yourself one. Or more.

Choosing a Mentor

Mentoring relationships involve people, and people need to gel if they are to have a mutually satisfactory relationship. And you can't gel with everyone. Whether you and your mentor are successful as a team depends on what you both expect from the relationship and whether your experience and personality characteristics allow you both to achieve your aims. For mentors have aims in mentoring you, as well as the other way round. But from your point of view you first have to know where you are heading and who can help you get there.

There is an irony in choosing a mentor: you are trying to exercise the kind of judgement about your potential mentors which you hope contact with your mentor will develop in you. Daft, isn't it? You can, however, help yourself by asking, and answering, a series of questions. The following list is taken from Hennig and Jardim:

- Where am I now?
- What is my present level of knowledge, skill and competence?
- Who are the people I know?
- What positions do they hold?
- What can they help me with?
- What can they teach me?
- What information do they have that I need?
- Whom do they know who can help me? (p160)

When you have answered these questions as fully as you can,

you have to survey the field available to see who can best suit your purposes. Watch the way people in your organisation and other networks help other people, listen to their problems, encourage them, give them hints, etc. Talk about this with colleagues and listen to their assessment of others to help you build up a picture so that you can judge for yourself whether certain people could help you up your career ladder. Try and judge from a basis of informed opinion. Intuition, even women's, isn't always right. But equally, don't undervalue gut feelings. If you are uncomfortable being alone in the same room as a potential mentor, then there is something seriously wrong. You might be able to develop a working relationship with that person, but it is doubtful whether a good mentoring relationship could result. A mentoring relationship need not involve the revelation of personal confidences, but it does require mutual trust and often becomes emotionally close, so anyone who makes you uncomfortable should not be chosen as your mentor.

Some organisations have mentoring schemes and you have a more or less restricted choice of mentor. For example, some organisations just assign mentors to you, while in other cases you are able to choose from a list of mentors the one that you would prefer. Some people are popular as mentors, and are oversubcribed, so you may have to accept your second choice. In these cases where choice is limited you will doubtless try and get the most you can from the mentor that you get, but always remember that you could ask someone else to be your mentor as well, perhaps informally from within your organisation or from one of your other networks. And you might have more than one mentor at any one time, or at different stages in your career, to meet your changing needs.

Harriet's experience demonstrates what can happen with official schemes unless they are thought out very carefully. Her company operated a mentoring scheme for trainee managers, but she and her mentor came together by 'sheer chance'. They found their way to each other through 'the limited grapevine. There was no real evaluation or thought given to anything other than ensuring trainees were [paired] with senior "influential" managers in their field of work.' In other words, her organisation, a very large nationalised industry, was interested in 'pairing' people up, but not in 'matching' them properly. No attention was paid to ensuring that the mentor and mentee matched each other's needs in terms of career development and personal growth. The quality of the mentoring that resulted was left very much to chance, and Harriet's experiences with her official mentor were not altogether happy ones. This obliged her to look for other people to give her the help she was not getting from her official mentor. As she says, 'I did . . . form several informal, short-term mentoring relationships with senior managers during my career. They were very varied in their quality and "use".'

In other organisations where there is no formal system of mentoring you will have to go hunting to find someone who suits your current needs best.

Characteristics to Look For

In a handbook for the training of mentors I found the following list of characteristics that a mentor should possess: 'patient, firm, caring, fair, good listener, good communicator, persuasive, manipulative, encouraging, committed, enthusiastic, trust-worthy, honest, good humoured – as well as having a sense of humour, empathy, logical, respected, positive, creative, imaginative' (Local Government Training Board, 1985).

Most of these are characteristic of people with good interpersonal or teaching skills. The only one that relates to a person's professional standing is 'respected'. This may be explained by the fact that this handbook had been written for people (Education Officers) who were already judged to be good at their craft. They were now to induct and oversee the development of new Education Officers.

Other articles and books about mentoring talk a great deal about the characteristics which reveal the high professional standing of mentors, like: successful, very influential, senior manager, respected, well-liked, knows the business, knows everybody, gets what he wants, still going up.

In putting this book together I relied on my own experience, that of friends and colleagues, and my reading on the subject. But I also supplemented this with a survey of women previously unknown to me and their experiences of mentors. They initially filled in a questionnaire and we later corresponded by letter or phone. Most of them had responded to a request for help sent out to members of Women in Management, but later other women volunteered too. I asked them what characteristics they had found useful in their mentor. It is interesting to look at what they said, and to compare it with the lists above. They listed the following, in this order:

1. Ability to teach or facilitate learning
2. Wide network of contacts
3. Willingness to share experience
4. Professional/academic qualifications
5. Sharpness of intellect
6. Ability to think on their feet
7. Ability to give advice and then withdraw
8. Organisational skills
9. Wisdom
10. Success
11. Influence
12. Discretion
13. Perception
14. Commitment to the development of young people

At other points in their response they also mentioned the following:

- Good listener
- Their willingness to use their time on my behalf
- The teaching of confidence-building and believing in oneself
- Enthusiasm
- Patience
- Absolute confidence in own ability
- Role-model attributes
- Professional entrepreneur
- Shrewd but direct
- Very direct
- Very high standards
- Skills purchase

Whilst no statistical significance is claimed for these responses, it is worth noting that the characteristics they found useful and desirable are a mixture of people and professional attributes, to use a rough division, with the people skills being rather more preponderant.

My respondents were also invited to comment on the characteristics that they found most *important*. Again they commented on a mixture of characteristics, but their fullest comments concerned teaching and networks contacts. Of the mentor's teaching ability they particularly liked being allowed to learn in their own way, without being forced into any particular behaviour. These comments are representative: 'She has well-honed communication skills. She has the ability to share her experiences and her knowledge base, in a manner that facilitates learning. She plants ideas and then waits for them to germinate on their own.' One person talked of 'often [being] thrown in at the deep end', but realising that this was an opportunity to learn.

One woman disliked many of the characteristics of her mentor. He was indiscreet, unreliable and erratic in his attention to his mentees, and not intellectually very bright. But his wide network of contacts and his great influence over others proved their value in her case: as his mentee she had access to these networks and spheres of influence and thus gained visibility and credibility within her company and outside it. She now gives frequent conference papers, achieving even more credibility.

In the main the priorities shown in these lists do not surprise me. If you are to learn from people, it is best if they have good communication and people skills. And since you are likely to develop quite a close (if not intimate) relationship you need to be sure that they are discreet and trustworthy. But these priorities are different from those generally revealed in the literature, where many more professional skills are listed, and are given a higher priority. I suspect that is because most of the work reported elsewhere has been done with men as well as women, whereas my survey concentrates on women. Reich has noted the same thing:

> Female mentor-protégé relationships were different from those involving men only. The affective, or emotional, quality was more vital for women than men. . . . Women, like men, emphasize the professional nature of mentoring, but as women they are more likely than men to stress the caring, nurturing, and teaching aspects of the relationship (*The Mentor Connection*, pp53–54).

There is plenty of evidence from psychology research to show that women are more concerned about the 'quality' of their relationships than what their relationships can bring them. Women should be alert to this when they are choosing their mentors. They have to make up their own minds what they want, and seek out the mentor whose characteristics will best suit them, their immediate and their ultimate goals.

What did initially surprise me was that 'a commitment to the development of junior people' came last of all in the rank order. But then I realised that this is perhaps not so difficult to explain. A higher placing could have indicated that the mentors in these relationships were really people with a burning zeal to educate, regardless of revealed talent. But if we take together the lowest and the highest characteristic, that they were able to teach or facilitate learning without obviously being committed to the development of junior people, this suggests that they were good facilitators of learning for those they thought worth the effort, who had a good chance of climbing a long way up the ladder, and who had the ability to work with them. Perhaps this shows efficiency in the use of their teaching skills?

A Word of Warning

The warning to be drawn from this, therefore, is not just to look for someone who can teach you. Make sure that the person you choose also has the knowledge and experience that you want to have passed on to you.

And perhaps it would be wise to add a word here too about 'successful' people acting as mentors. It is generally assumed that their very success makes them eligible. But the respondents in my survey put 'success' more than half-way down the list of desirable characteristics. One respondent who had no mechanisms to guide her, and therefore had a free hand in choosing her mentor, did not choose one who was flamboyantly successful in the whizz-kid sense. Instead she chose someone with 'a long track record of management' in the company she was in, and in the area she was hoping to move into permanently. Her thinking here was that his long track record had given him experience in all those areas where she was likely to want help or guidance; he had been there before; he knew the organisation inside out. In that he had made progress, he did not have enemies strong enough to have prevented his climb. Being attached to him would therefore be safe. She was not hitching herself to someone controversial. Who might be fun, but not safe.

Indeed it may sometimes be sensible to take as a mentor some-one who has made steady progress, but perhaps not to the highest levels, who knows that she will never get there because of aspects of her own personality or own skill bank (or age, particularly in the case of a woman who has taken time out), but who is nevertheless a person of discernment, who knows what it takes to get to the top, and will have the generosity to help you climb beyond her.

For 'successful' people can be unsafe as mentors. They may have reached certain stages in the organisation because they fitted in with, were approved by, those in power up to that stage. But they might not make it to the next stage up, for several reasons: their face may not fit at that level, or a boardroom revolution may take place and new directions may be required which they don't or can't follow. And then what happens to their mentees who have been riding on cloud nine with them?

If you are in the unfortunate position of having a mentor who has fallen from grace, find another one quick. This may sound cynical, but it is reality. Mentors who are not in favour are not going to be of any further use to you as mentors, at least not in that organisation. Sticking to them out of loyalty is not going to help you, unless there is some real point of principle at stake on which you will not give. Only you can judge. And if a personal relation-ship has developed with your mentor, you can still continue that side of your relationship, but do find someone else who can help you in your career. The rules of supply and demand operate in mentoring just as in any other aspect of the business world. You buy from the person who is offering the goods you want, at the price you are prepared to pay. If the goods you want, namely help in climbing up the ladder, are no longer on offer, don't continue to pay for them. If your mentor no longer fulfils your mentoring needs, go to another supplier.

In any case, you should periodically ask yourself what you want of your mentoring relationship and whether your needs are being met. And if they are not, you should change mentors. A stale mentoring relationship is no good. It needs to be challenging, energising and productive. If not, look elsewhere.

One or More Mentors?
There is absolutely no reason why you should have only one men-tor. One respondent volunteered that the first thing she does when

moving into a new job is find a new mentor. She doesn't discard the old ones, but their relationship takes on a different quality, since they no longer have direct day-to-day influence over her development. And different mentors may be needed at different times, or even simultaneously.

For example, even if your company has assigned you a mentor with whom you generally feel comfortable and happy, it may be that that mentor has never experienced something that is very important to you, like caring for children or relatives. Many women have such responsibilities and sometimes find it difficult to balance the demands of work and home. The emotional strain of leaving at home a child or elderly relative who may be ill or in some other sort of distress, can cause serious lack of concentration or even crises of identity and self-worth. Your mentor may be sympathetic, but you may feel that she is unable to help in practical terms from her own experience.

Try and find someone, in your own organisation if you wish, but perhaps from your wider networks, who does know how difficult this can be, and talk to her about it. No one can solve that problem for you, but someone could tell you how she managed to deal with a similar situation herself. And how comforting it is to hear someone else who has trodden the same path reassure you that you are not losing your commitment to your job and your career just because occasionally your conditioning gets to you and you feel that as a loving mother (or daughter) you really should (or indeed may prefer to) stay home and nurse the children yourself.

Male or Female Mentor?
Do you, as a woman, want a man or woman as your mentor? Donald Bowen researched this question of cross-gender mentoring, and gave his results in a number of published and unpublished papers. He started from the popular view that mentoring works best where the protégé(e) 'identifies' with the mentor, and that female/female relationships are likely to be more mutually profitable, since women are assumed to identify better with other women. He examined the predictive value of this view with the help of 32 successful mentoring pairs and essentially came to the conclusion that there was no clear difference between the degree of identification felt between female/female and male/female pairs. He concluded that it is the function that the mentor per-

forms, rather than his or her sex that is the key factor in the success of mentoring ('Were Men Meant to Mentor Women?').

This entirely concurs with my own views of the matter, based on the experience of more than twenty years and the comments of my respondents. It depends entirely on what you want out of the mentoring relationship. I have seen many perfectly successful relationships where women have had male mentors, and vice versa. I have also had and continue to have male mentees, and have personally never come across a *problem* related to our different sex. The subject is often mentioned, but usually in a semi-joking sense like, 'That is a typically male reaction. If only you men would learn that pulling rank is not the best way to handle people . . .' and no damage is done.

The respondents in my survey had men and women as mentors, and several had mentors of both sexes. Their networks had brought them into contact with a range of people who could serve their purposes at different times and they had chosen according to needs and availability at any one time. None of them commented specifically on whether in general terms they preferred to be mentored by men or women, though some of them had experienced certain problems in cross-gender relationships.

I would also refer sceptics to Hennig and Jardim whose book *The Managerial Woman* analysed the progress of 25 very successful women who had identified with and been mentored by men (though the word 'mentor' is not used).

In finding a mentor just choose the person who seems to you to have most of the characteristics you are looking for, and fewest of those you want to avoid. And supplement your needs with other people.

For example, if you are looking for a mentor in your own organisation you may have little choice of gender, since there are still many more men than women in senior positions. In particular, if you are a lone women working among men you might have a male mentor in your company, but you might also want to find a lone woman mentor, someone who knows how isolated you can occasionally feel because of the strong male culture all around you. In this case you have to rely on your networks. Always ask for help. Most people are happy to be asked. And most people are happy to help. Especially women. Women are very supportive of other women. Use them.

Initiating Contact

If you are involved in a formal mentoring scheme either in your place of work or your networks, the initiation of contact is planned for you. Someone will tell you when and where to turn up, and you work from there. The situation is different where no formal system exists. Of the people I have spoken to who have had informal mentoring, none can remember exactly how the relationship started. The initial contact has usually been in a meeting of some kind with other people. They remember talking to their future mentors in general terms, and at some stage being asked about themselves, how they were getting on, what their plans were. They also remember chatting over coffee, and suddenly finding themselves asking for advice or guidance, like: 'By the way, I've heard that you worked in the Windsor office for a while. I've been asked if I would consider going out there. I was wondering whether you could give me some idea of what I might be faced with?' In other cases they have made contact on the phone, sometimes after speaking face to face, but as often as not because someone else had suggested giving someone a ring, 'because she knows about that sort of thing.' And then the relationship just seemed to grow from there. This underlines the importance we attached earlier to networking, getting yourself involved with a wide range of groups that will allow you to locate the people potentially important to your future, and to allow them to notice you.

Although there is a widespread rumour about going up to people and saying 'Will you mentor me?' (and indeed there exists a slightly wicked cartoon about a young man asking a senior woman to mentor him), I have never found anyone who claims that her mentoring relationship started remotely like that. The people concerned just grew together.

Being Chosen

We have noted that mentoring partners often just come together. But some women report being specifically picked out and chosen by their mentors. Something in them tells their potential mentors that they are people of talent, and worth developing. Beth says 'My mentor personally offered to train me.' This was very unusual in her company, a large nation-wide recruitment consultancy. Despite its size and reputation, her company did not have a mentoring policy, and even informal mentoring was rarely seen. So she was lucky. Her mentoring took her from being a secretary with little autonomy to being a junior consultant with the company. Later she set up her own consultancy.

Sandra was also specifically chosen. She worked for a much smaller organisation, a company letting land for car parking, but the owner knew development potential when he saw it. He wanted to expand and he knew that he could do so by giving her her head. He gave her extraordinary responsibility very soon after she joined the company, watching over her and teaching her the operational side of the business on the way. She very soon achieved her child-hood ambition of being financially secure.

And Sheila Needham was also picked out, though she demurs about saying this since her boss/mentor encouraged everyone, not just herself. She sees though, with hindsight, that theirs was a mentoring relationship. It was his faith in her abilities and his pushing her to achieve that gave her the experience she needed to develop her own confidence to go off and do her own thing.

Getting the Most out of Your Mentor

So having chosen your mentor, or been chosen, you now have to get the most out of her. It is, of course, true that your mentor will be looking at you, assessing your strengths and weaknesses, providing you with opportunities for growth, giving you appropriate praise or help. But you should also be looking at you and helping yourself to grow. So take the initiative into your own hands and use your mentor actively, getting the most you can out of this important aid to your development.

Your Mentor and You

Firstly, do make sure that you use your sessions with your mentor to the best advantage, and prepare for them too. This is not only so that you don't waste her time or yours, but so that you are increasingly seen to be someone who is thoughtful, sensitive, well-prepared, efficient, ambitious, in charge of her own destiny, etc. Whether you have occasional *ad hoc* meetings with your mentor, or regular and formal meetings imposed by the structure of the company mentoring scheme, the same principles apply: think in advance of what you want to say, comment on or seek help with, and take a note of these things with you to the meeting. And if there are several ways of tackling a problem which you have encountered, outline the various solutions and ask which solution your mentor would recommend. She may in fact recommend an approach you hadn't thought of, but by putting forward alternative lines of action, you demonstrate that you have the ability to think and the desire to do the job properly, not that you are asking someone else to do the job for you. Your mentor is not meant to do your thinking for you, but to help you develop.

It may be that in the mentoring scheme of your company sessions with your mentor are regular and perhaps based on a set agenda. There is some merit in this: it provides a sensible control mechanism to make sure you and your mentor don't drift apart, and it seeks to ensure that specific points of a mentee's development are discussed with her. This system can, however, be restrictive, implying that there is a 'best' way of mentoring, and that only those subjects on the official agenda are appropriate for discussion. If this system suits you, fine. If it doesn't, do something about it.

For example, if there is something that you could with profit discuss before the next scheduled mentoring meeting, ask for an extra meeting, perhaps a brief chat during the lunch period. Don't feel guilty about this. Remember that you and your mentor and the company are in this together. The company is mentoring you, devoting the time and energies of a senior person to your development, because you are worth mentoring. So ask for the help you need. It is to the benefit of everyone.

And ask for help when you need it. Obviously you will be sensible and not ask for an urgent meeting if the matter for discussion isn't really urgent, but ask for an appointment within a reasonable period of time. Take the initiative. Get a diary out and suggest a few dates. You will certainly get extra brownie points for thus being seen to be serious about your own development and hence about your value to the company.

And because mentoring can bring you immediate and longer-term benefits, it would be a terrible waste to forget what you have once learned. Keeping an on-going record is a good way of getting the most from the learning opportunities that your mentor provides. This could be just a running journal sort of thing, but it could also be an elaborated table with categories which you tick for what you have done or learned that day or week. It can be a manual record system, or you may like to put in on your computer, in which case you can have all sorts of useful cross referencing. Whichever system you choose, you should make sure you record the right things. Don't just write down the events, but also make a note of the lesson you have learned. For example an entry could read something like this:

> Went with EA to budgetting meeting. Met Treasurer (hates smoking). Learned that whenever EA spoke she leaned forward and raised her pencil seconds before she started speaking, thus giving visual signal that she was breaking in. Bloggs from personnel never spoke. Sat with arms crossed entire time. Nobody took any notice of MO when he tried to talk uninvited. Very quiet voice drowned out by the others.

There are several advantages to keeping such a record. You are able to peruse it every so often and remind yourself of what you have learned, and in this way relearn it and also re-evaluate it, seeing it in the light of events since then. You can also quite impress yourself by the things you have packed in, and this should increase your self-confidence, an essential characteristic of people looking for promotion. You should also record the names and functions of people your mentor has introduced you to, or whom you have met through her agency. For all the reasons we have stated before, people are important. And when you have reason to contact them in the future it is helpful to remind them of how you met. Somehow or other you can find a (natural) way of saying '. . . on the occasion when Elizabeth Anderson introduced us'. They may have a dim recollection of you, but because they know her your approach will be treated seriously.

This sort of record is very important indeed for women who are planning to take time out for whatever reason, or who are obliged to because of illness or redundancy. It serves to remind them of what they did, and what they learned, and therefore gives them that extra boost that most women need when they set out to re-enter the job market. It also provides them with a list of people who could be useful to them in their job search.

Your Mentor as a Resource

Think of your mentor as a resource and use that resource to the maximum of its value. She is (probably) older then you, more senior than you, a living example of achievement, confirmation that women can achieve the kind of success that you are after, and maybe a bit more. Having been there before you and done it all before, she has a lot to pass on to you. The respondents in my survey had used their mentors 'as an in-house consultant, to provide nuts and bolts factual knowledge – how to handle discipline, how to develop people, how to handle disputes' etc. Even her mistakes can increase the value of her advice to you.

Don't only listen to what advice she has to offer you. Ask for it. For example, you may have experienced some difficulty in fully understanding a particular report because of the financial detail in it, and you realise that you need to brush up on your financial knowledge. So discuss with your mentor this particular weakness, and ask how you can improve, for example by reading, going on courses, or undertaking some specific study. Your mentor will help you to decide how important this area is to you at the moment, in terms of your own development, and the company's needs of you. Perhaps something else should be given greater priority which you haven't noticed because you do not have your mentor's perspective. But if your mentor agrees that this is an important area at this time, she can suggest those routes to improvement which will benefit you and the company. You might not actually need a course at all. A short secondment to a finance section may be all you need, for your present purposes.

This example is particularly important for women. Despite active efforts by educationists and women's organisations girls are, in general, still not brought up to take an interest in finance, nor are they sufficiently encouraged to study mathematical or financial subjects at school or university. Enlightened women therefore, knowing that this is likely to be an area where they are weak, may well try to compensate. They may put considerable effort into improving their financial knowledge, and may possibly do more than is necessary for the job, when it would be more beneficial to concentrate on something else at this stage.

Don't just use your mentor as a source of advice, either. Use her also to provide information which she has or can obtain easily

75

because of her status and experience. If you need to put together some statistics in a recommendation you are writing, give her a ring. Don't assume you have to spend ages tracking down the information yourself. You could, but should you? You could spend three hours combing through a library. But why re-invent the wheel when it would be much less time-consuming to ask your mentor what the best source is of the information you need? Indeed she may already have the information to hand. What I am proposing is not that you cheat, but that you be efficient. Your mentor has been using her own sources for years. Let her show you the short cuts.

Another way in which you can use your mentor as a resource is to ask her to arrange to get you experience in certain areas you feel you are missing out on. For example, you could have heard on the grapevine (using your networks again) that your company is considering direct marketing as a way of expanding its markets. You know that companies similar to yours are doing this, but you realise that you don't know very much about it. Mention your interest to your mentor, and the fact that you feel you should know more about the field. It would be even more productive if you did a bit of work first and found out that a conference would be taking place on the subject the next month. You could then ask whether she thinks it would be a good idea for you to attend. She may not, and may just suggest that you read up about the subject. But direct marketing is a rapidly developing area, so she may approve of your attendance at the conference and authorise it. She may even pull a few strings to get you there, especially in view of your positively expressed interest in improving your knowledge to the benefit of the company. In this way, you get to meet the people active in developing this technique; you can ask for information of direct relevance to your company's operations, and get a response straight from the horse's mouth.

And by asking to attend the conference you also receive several additional benefits you probably hadn't bargained for. You also get the opportunity to increase your networks and visibility. And since the proper use of such an opportunity is very important to your career you are obviously going to say or ask something intelligent so that you are remembered by the people present, those who could be directly and indirectly instrumental in your promotion.

Or your mentor might suggest that you attend the conference with someone from the marketing department who is going anyway. She can arrange this for you, while you might not yet have the authority to suggest such a thing yourself. Or she might be going to the conference anyway, and decide to take you along with her. In these latter two instances you are also being given a public seal of approval, a sort of 'presentation at court'. By being seen in the company of senior people who obviously consider it worthwhile spending time and money on you, you are marked down as someone with a future, someone to take note of. You are again increasing your networks and your visibility, but this time with the added bonus. And do remember to use this as a learning experience. Watch how your mentor operates with other people, greeting them, recalling previous encounters, asking after colleagues, showing an informed interest in the latest developments, giving out a little bit of business gossip, latest appointments, etc. All these things are desperately important to the development of your own networking skills.

Similarly, you can ask for experience to allow you to learn important lessons about the way your company operates. For example, you could say that you really don't understand what happens when a factory inspection is carried out, and is there any chance that you might go on one? In this way, having expressed an interest, you are likely to be intelligent and useful company on the next inspection visit your mentor makes. Or she might arrange for you to go on a visit with a senior colleague. Either way you increase your networks, your visibility, and public knowledge about your seal of approval. If you had not asked, it may have been a long time before you got round to doing this.

And this sort of 'being in tow' is also vitally important inside the company, to show the people of influence that you are considered worth watching. You may tell your mentor that you don't quite understand how the proposal to which you contributed the statistics is going to be handled at the next stage up. She could arrange for you to attend the relevant meeting with the person presenting the proposal. She could even arrange for you to talk to the particular part of the proposal in which you had a hand. This is extremely important exposure, bringing you to the attention of people who might otherwise not know of your existence. It also brings them to your attention, so that the next time you meet in the corridor, the carpark or wherever, you can sensibly pass the time of day, maintaining your presence in the forefront of their minds.

The important thing about all this is to use your mentor actively. The more you ask the more you are likely to be given.

Your Mentor as a Confidante

If you are finding something really rather difficult, talk to your mentor about it. Just having someone listen to your problems often helps you to solve them as you relate them. But there may be something concrete that she can do to help.

I remember one of my mentees telling me that she felt under extreme pressure from a new member of her staff. She felt him to be constantly critical and supercilious, and found it hard to have a rational discussion with him when he came into her room. We talked around the subject for quite a while, for there were obviously things wrong with her attitude to this young man. His behaviour was not without fault, but it did not merit the reaction she was showing. And she knew it. Eventually our breakthrough came when she exploded 'But Lily, he's so big!' I was being serious when I asked, 'Have you ever asked him to sit down?' She stared in astonishment and replied that she didn't think she ever had. All she needed to do was lessen the physical inequality of their respective sizes for her to be able to behave rationally to him without feeling threatened all the time.

This analysis of the situation took no great genius on my part. I was able to help merely because I could look at all the factors objectively without the emotional bias which had been building up. But I would not have been able to help her if she had not come to me.

A group of women for whom confidential moral support is vital is women returners. They all need help in getting into the different gear that they will need when they return to work. Even women who have been extremely successful before taking a career break lose a sense of their own capacity and self-worth. One friend of mine ran her own multi-million-pound business before selling up and having a two-year break. But her trepidation on taking up paid employment again would have been funny had it not been so serious to her. She confided to me that she was appalled by the amount of paper that she was expected to read, digest and be ready to comment on before a meeting. She genuinely believed that she had lost the ability to do this!

Your Mentor and Your Future

Discussing with your mentor what your next career move might be should be easy enough if she is not in your own organisation. It is a little more tricky if you are both in the same organisation and you have become mutually dependent, or if she has been grooming you for progression specifically in that company. But it can still be done if you approach the subject with tact and sensitivity, saying that you are really a little bit concerned about your position in the company at the moment, and that you would appreciate her advice about what you could expect in the near future. You are, after all, alerting her to your concerns, and she may be able to resolve them in terms beneficial to you, herself and the company.

From working closely with you for a while she will have a fair idea of you and your capabilities, can also help you see the whole of your career in perspective, and can discuss with you the options you have at any one time. You may be ready for promotion, but there may just simply be no slot for you to fit in. The company may not be developing at the moment, and may have a full complement of people able to manage it appropriately. Is it better to bide your time in the company, so that you will be in place when policies change or someone else moves on, or should you move on elsewhere and get experience of different companies, their methods and their cultures, possibly with the intention of coming back to your present company when the circumstances look right?

She will help you think whether you want to stay in the same company, the same field, or whether you should alter somewhat. For example, if you are a dentist in a hospital, is now the time to look for a higher level job but still in a hospital, or do you want to go into general practice? Or do you want to apply for a teaching post? Or maybe, whatever career you are in, you suspect that you are not really suited in the long run to this area of work, and you would like to discuss with your mentor whether and how you might change.

Career change is more common for women than men, often because women have gone into jobs which really do not stretch them adequately. Your mentor can help you assess your chances of success in an entirely different career. One of the more altruistic acts of my life was performed when I was acting as mentor to one of my secretaries. She was a wonderful secretary, but I encouraged her desire to leave and train as a probation officer. I missed her terribly, but she is now a much more fulfilled being. Yve Newbold has done the same thing. Yve, who is the Company Secretary of the industrial conglomerate, Hanson, has always encouraged younger colleagues. Five of her secretaries have profited from this encouragement, and have successfully changed careers moving into, for example, law and publishing (see Colback and Maconochie).

If the time does come for you to move on and you decide to look for another job, do seek the advice of your mentor. At the very least ask if you can give her as a referee in your application. You may not yet be well-known, but you will be considered worth looking at if she has agreed to sponsor you.

Better still, enlist your mentor's help in your job search. As we have already noted, many jobs are filled without public advertisement, and she may well know of something suitable. She may even suggest that you write 'on spec' to such and such a company. In which case, with her permission, you will start your letter with something like 'I am writing at the suggestion of Elizabeth Anderson.' And if you have any wit about you, you will also ask her to give the individual concerned a ring beforehand, and coordinate the arrival of your letter with her phone call, so that your approach is positively anticipated. She may ring up off her own bat anyway, but it does not harm to prompt her. This merely shows that you know how the world goes round, and people who don't don't get good jobs.

Looking After Your Mentor

There is an entirely different aspect to getting the most out of your mentor. Mentoring is about relationships. Like any other relationship it needs to be nurtured and handled with care to give benefit to all parties. Nobody is going to give generously of her time and experience, even if it is part of her job description, unless she gets something in return. That something could be very simple, like the pleasure of your stimulating company. She may occasionally just enjoy relaxing with you, going for a drink, going shopping, visiting a museum. I have done such things with my mentees and know others who do the same. This is a way of cementing a bond, tending a relationship that both mentor and protégée consider important and to some extent privileged. But you as a mentee must respect this privilege. In such relaxed circumstances people reveal things about themselves that they would not wish to have repeated. They may, for example, reveal weaknesses in their own behaviour to help you overcome similar problems. It is therefore essential that you learn to receive and respect confidences. People who let others down are unlikely to be recommended.

But your mentor could also get other returns from having you as a mentee, things more clearly work-orientated. For example, if she arranges a special visit for you, it is both smart and courteous to write up a critical report and give her a copy, thus keeping her in touch with developments for little outlay of time or energy. Or you could provide her with the latest information on a certain matter. Supposing she mentioned in conversation that she had heard a piece on the radio that morning about the use of bonuses in retaining staff; you could reply that that was something you worked on for your college dissertation, and you could discuss your findings with her, offering to let her see a copy. In this way she benefits from having you as her mentee and feels justified in the amount of time she is taking over you. And is consequently better disposed to you and will be more active and generous (and useful) in her mentoring.

Sarah Knight

Sarah is very successful. She runs the computer sales division of a large multinational. But it was not always like this. There is no doubt in her mind that she owes this success to her mentor, a woman who totally transformed her attitudes, values and way of living.

At the time they met, Sarah was in the United States. She had recently completed a Master of Science degree, but was now unemployed and drifting aimlessly. She calls it 'leading a nomadic existence'. She was introduced to her mentor by a male friend who thought they had a few things in common. They met briefly, then the mentor phoned up and suggested lunch. And things went on from there.

Sarah was 27 years old, her mentor seventeen years her senior. Gradually her mentor helped Sarah to see herself in a new light, to break free from the conditioning which taught her that progress could only be achieved by relying on male associates. She began to believe in herself and her potential, and with the help of her mentor worked out a career plan.

After Sarah's return to the UK, it took her only four years to achieve complete financial independence. She now has an enormous sense of relief at finally being able to dictate the pace of her own life.

Sarah is a bit in awe of her mentor. She describes her as 'professional, with a wide circle of contacts; a superior intellect, eminently wise and successful, totally discreet and trustworthy. She can share her knowledge and experience in a way that facilitates learning: she plants ideas and then waits for them to germinate on their own.'

Her mentor taught Sarah things of direct importance to her future career, such as introducing her to information technology, teaching her business methods, alerting her to office politics and showing her how to handle them. But she also taught her things of general life importance. They often discussed environmental issues, and other topics of the day, even aspects of nutrition. And together they examined feminist theory and history. In this way Sarah was able to move away from female stereotypes and expand her horizons. She also improved her communication skills, in particular her use of language.

Sarah recognises that her mentor has been selfless in her advice and guidance. 'I might add that she takes an enormous delight in my progress and humorously acknowledges the credit that is due to her. Our relationship has a unique and special aspect to it.'

CHAPTER 4

The Benefits of Being Mentored

There are several ways mentors help their mentees: they provide support, protection, opportunities for growth and learning, facilities, feedback, information, knowledge of organisational politics, and they act as role models. Kram, amongst others, has noted in 'Phases of the Mentor Relationship' that the precise benefits of being mentored depend on the different needs of the mentee at any one stage of development. One of the aims of my survey of women who had been mentored was to find out what kind of help they had received, what they had learned from their mentoring, and what they had achieved as a result. The rest of this chapter relies heavily on the comments they made, and in several instances I have lifted their wording wholesale from the information they sent me.

My respondents listed what they had learned with help from their mentors. Although all these skills were listed in relation to employment, many of them have implications beyond the world of work. To give an overview, I have grouped them under headings, but some skills could fit into several categories.

Improving Performance
Watch and learn from other people's strategies.
Learn from others without copying blindly.
Get the same effect as others but using different strategies.
Isolate factors, and give reasoned response.
Solve problems rather than complain about problems.
Learn to take calculated risks.
Use all available resources.
Seek and use advice.

Make requests.
Utilise specific skills.
Handle committees.
Organise.

Technical Skills
Write a report.
Make oral presentations.
Perform option appraisals.
Handle meetings.
Chair meetings.
Service meetings.
Manage projects.
Consult.
Negotiate – learning how to create a win/win situation.
Draw up budgets.
Learn forward planning.
Prepare for events.
Prepare business method.
Analyse problems.
Develop selling skills.
Learn assessment skills.
Learn decision-making skills.

Career Development
Plan career.
Find out more about the job.
Make an impression at meetings.
Speak up at meetings.
Increase personal visibility.
Develop personal credibility.
Get new training.
Maximise training.
Transfer learning from one area to another.
Dress appropriately.
Understand company structure better.
Get promotion.
Increase power.
Increase assertiveness.

Recognise that personal humility may not be appropriate.
Increase influence.
Work the system.

Handling People

Dealing with aggression and difficult situations.
Handling management of people.
Be creative in leadership.
Welcome creativity of other people.
Take people with you when you lead them.
Improve inter-personal communication.
Improve long-distance communication with others.
Improve long-term communication with others.
Network.
Listen to grapevine.
Provide leadership.
Compromise.
Save face.
Apologise.
Deal with cross-gender aggression, jealousy and sexual harassment.
Deal with suspicion from other colleagues.

Personal Growth

Become aware of nutrition.
Develop environmental awareness.
Be proud of my accomplishments.
To move away from female stereotypes.
Enrich vocabulary, syntax.
Discuss feminist theory and history.
Become more confident.
Take responsibility for self.
Develop personal skills.
Become more assertive.
Remain within own personality but make progress.
Act with personal integrity.
Combat isolation.
Explore limitations of personal mindset.
Become interested in feminism.
Take interest in topics of the day.

85

Balance of Home and Career
Get perspective on job and career.
Obtain success without sacrificing personal life.
Cope with conflict of work and domestic responsibilities.

What these lists show is that some things are specific to individual jobs, others relate to the company environment, and yet others help the mentee grow as an employee and as a person.

Job-Specific Benefits

Mentors can give you specific help with new tasks. A woman who has produced many well-known radio series told me of the technical help her mentor gave her when she had her first production assignments. He went through every script she wrote for the first year, querying various points, saying 'No, they won't understand that' when she wasn't getting her points across and rewriting them with her.

In that job writing was absolutely fundamental, and had to be right, otherwise the mentee would make no further progress. The mentor knew that his mentee was good, but she had a weakness that had to be dealt with, and he helped her get over it.

But writing skills are fundamental to most management jobs, even in engineering, where for example the attention senior people give to a new proposal depends very much on how the junior person presents that proposal. The engineering skills have to be there. But so does the writing, and mentors will see that you pay attention to this as well for the benefit of your future development.

Financial sophistication is also vital. Some jobs like accountancy rely on financial skills, but an understanding of financial matters is essential to the running of any department, in profit- or non-profit-making concerns. And people who become self-employed soon realise the importance of financial control. One mentor admitted to me that she felt her own earlier progress had been impeded by not having enough confidence in financial matters. I found this hard to believe since she was promoted to a directorship in a large manufacturing company! So she always makes sure that her mentees have adequate financial awareness, and gives them their own budget at the earliest opportunity. In this way they learn financial planning and budgetary control, while being protected by her overall control if real danger threatens.

Computer literacy is another such basic requirement essential for today's employees and tomorrow's leaders. Unless you specialise in computers, for example in hardware engineering, you do not need a detailed knowledge of how computers work. But you must be able to appreciate the function of computers in your job, company and profession. If you are not comfortable with the way computers are used in your area, your mentor will make sure that you go on courses, or spend time in the appropriate department to get your understanding up to scratch.

Committee skills and negotiating skills are essential virtually everywhere, and many mentees report the help that they got from their mentors by being taken into meetings with them, where they would otherwise have had no place, to watch or learn how people behaved. One mentee reports that it was particularly important for her to learn how to create win/win situations in which everyone feels she has won something from the negotiation, and others who have been defeated are still left with a sense of self-worth.

And knowledge of some areas of the law is essential for people with supervisory or managerial responsibility. A sense of legal liability is something even non-lawyers mention a lot, knowing what can go wrong for a company if the staff, customers or shareholders are not satisfied.

These then are typical of job skills required in any person seeking promotion beyond the lowest levels, no matter what company or area you work in, from running a school to producing biscuits, and mentors ensure that they are learned.

Company-Specific Benefits

Other benefits of mentoring relate to the behaviour appropriate in a given company, regardless of specific job skills. This is what is called company culture, and applies to everything from the colour of your tights, your managerial style, to the car you should drive. And the value attached to these things varies from company to company, so the help of an insider is pretty important. It is vital to adopt the company style or you will not fit in, or be seen to fit in, and you will not be promoted. Your mentor can advise you in the company idiosyncracies, sometimes in very small details, but details which have important ramifications. Sargent gives an example of such advice, demonstrating that one woman's speech habits were a problem in a particular company:

> Frequently, they also express their feelings before stating their opinions or solutions, and so appear pokey [sic] to respond. A male manager trying to coach a new female manager said: 'You're just not thinking fast enough, or putting your ideas out quickly enough for our culture here. By the time you get part way through what you're saying people will be thinking of what else they have to do, drumming on their pads with pencils, or staring out of the window' (p21).

No one is going to get far in this particular company unless she can alter her pace of delivery, for no one is going to take time to listen for the points she might eventually make. A mentor can make sure that her mentee is sent on courses to improve this aspect of her behaviour, or she can coach her herself, getting her to argue with her, and reformulating her language and delivery until she gets into the company stride. Or advise her to look for work elsewhere.

I was recently given a marvellous example of company culture by a recruitment manager in the London office of an international finance house. What he actually said to me was: 'And we do have very good sports facilities. We expect people who work for us to keep themselves fit. It is part of our image to be seen as wholesome.'

Now somehow this sounded odd. There are, after all, ways of keeping fit other than joining the firm's sports club. So why this insistence? Because there is here a hidden message which only the smart guys, those who can both listen and hear, would pick up, a message much more important than the obvious one. The hidden message runs: 'Our world-wide reputation depends on delivering a very high-quality product. We work to certain set standards and procedures. We have our own way of doing things and we expect you to conform. It costs us a lot to train you before we see any real returns for the company, and we want to be sure that you are worth the training. We want you to demonstrate acceptance and approval of our way of doing things.' By joining the sports club you are doing this. You demonstrate that you are going to fit in. You are worth training.

Conformity is important in this company. Conform you will or not stay long. Shortly after this meeting with the recruitment manager I learned from a mentor in that company that women have to have this message rammed home to them. They are expected to be seen at the sports club, instead of rushing off home to tend to their children or their husbands. And the women who want to advance do learn this lesson, and make attendance part of their commitment to their job. This company does in fact employ more women than normally found at senior levels. But they all stay late. They all conform.

Hennig and Jardim give another example of the kind of conforming behaviour expected by certain companies:

> In one company we know of the style demanded for junior
> executives is that of a loyal soldier and it is precise down to the
> details of the uniform – Gucci shoes. The men talk about them,
> laugh at them. But they buy them and wear them (p31).

I have also recently heard of a company in which the chairman of the board smokes a pipe. This is somewhat difficult for the health-conscious younger employees. Their compromise is to walk around in the corridors from office to office with an unlit, unstuffed pipe in their hand as a sign of acceptance and conformity. My informant couldn't remember seeing the women employees doing this.

General Benefits

Let us now look at some of the ways mentors offer help, whether they relate to job or company benefits, personal or career growth.

Role Model
It was certainly helpful to have someone skilled to copy, to be used as a 'model for how [you] can deal with other people in the organisation, how to conduct and handle yourself (*not* necessarily by telling but enabling you to find the best, acceptable and unacceptable methods available to you as an individual managing in

that particular organisation).' Or 'someone to '"teach" you how he/she operates when handling "X" situation so you see how he/she thinks/feels/acts in a 3-dimensional way (not simply talk).' One woman says that the major thing about her mentor is that she is positive about everything she does, her own work and her teaching of others. Several women make the point that you do not have to admire every single feature of a role model. You can copy from her those bits of behaviour that fit your personality and ignore the rest.

Several women say that they have used their role models to learn how to be mentors in their own right. One woman's experience was so good that she developed a 'desire to be in a position to do the same for someone else'.

Protection

Shielding a mentee from catastrophic consequences of mistakes was considered very important. One woman said she never had 'attacks of timidity in entrepreneurial situations because of my mentor's experience, contacts, knowledge and drive. I could do just what I wanted when I wanted to. I could screw up, but it didn't matter because he was always there to sort it out.' She certainly learned from being given such freedom, becoming financially independent and setting up her own business.

And plenty of us must have taken the responsibility for mistakes our mentees have made. In them it is judged as incompetence. We, being higher up the tree, can laugh it off as a slip, 'apologies all round', and we are forgiven.

Learning Opportunities

Contact with someone prepared to expose you to new learning experiences was much valued. One person mentioned 'having someone in the know to give you some help/advice about areas of learning needed; someone who can open doors for you and create opportunities to learn – but not in a patriarchal "preferential" way.' Another talked enthusiastically of 'learning in leaps and bounds and great gulps of practical experience'. She gained 'insights to the real "cut and thrust" of business life', for 'real-life experience was always available [to her] from one of the obvious best.' One woman, who was a junior trade-union officer, wanted to attend an internal disciplinary hearing to find out what the procedures were. This was a perfectly legitimate interest, but the rules didn't allow it as the man concerned already had someone to defend him, someone from head office. But her mentor was a canny soul. Knowing that she was skilled in sound recording he got her appointed to record the hearing. There she learned a lot about such matters, and rapidly developed her own skills of advocacy.

Dispassionate Feedback

It was clearly important to have someone who was 'detached', an 'independent observer', whom you could use as 'a "cross-check" in confidence' to provide self-knowledge and a chance for improvement. The mentor provided an 'opportunity to hear or receive feedback about one's performance and perceived perform-ance, to look at the effects one is having on other people; an opportunity to look, with help, at oneself and evaluate [those] skills going well and those needing further development.' Mentors provide 'an opportunity in a "safe" environment to re-evaluate and learn from experiences at work, and in a constructive way', and 'a safe place to talk through, and work through, difficulties and inconsistencies with a supportive and interested person.' And perhaps vital was 'an interested party to tell you the bad news as well as the good news.'

Sponsoring and Recommending

One of the most important benefits that a mentor can provide is to sponsor you, to put you forward in a way that demonstrates her faith in you, her belief that you are worth watching and develop-ing. Sponsoring can take various forms, and occur at several levels, as we have seen in earlier chapters. Sponsorship can be spontaneous on the part of the mentor, or can arise from a request for help from the mentee. But the basis of sponsorship is that a senior person whose judgement is trusted stands up for you, thus putting a seal of approval on you.

A woman who wanted to convert from a scientific stream to the management stream in her company was sponsored by her mentor to do an MBA course. This is a coveted professional award, the possession of which is reckoned to demonstrate the holder's ability to reach senior levels of management, and often at a fast rate. It demands a high level of intelligence and the commitment of con-siderable time and energy. It also costs a lot of money, and companies only pay the fees when they are convinced that the investment of time and money in their employee is going to pay dividends. Hence the recommendation of a trusted person is vital (see Dix).

Even outsiders can sponsor their mentees, making them more visible inside their company. I had been working with a woman in her mid-twenties for about eighteen months, helping her to plan her career and get the kind of training that would be helpful. She was underused in her current job and went through several down periods, often phoning me for advice and encouragement. Eventually, without prior consultation with me, she took a job with an international charity. This job was not exactly what she had been looking for, but she knew that it offered her great potential inside the organisation and beyond. I happened to know the director-general of the organisation, and wrote to him congratulating him on the perspicacity of the staff who had appointed her (he had not been involved), and underlining a few of her better qualities, saying in essence that she was someone worth developing. I also let her know that I had done this so that she could find an opportunity to remind him of our acquaintance when they met. It all worked beautifully. After five months, and several detailed interviews with the director-general, she was sent off to take up a foreign assignment. She is good, but we have no doubt it would have taken her longer to reach this stage if I had not sponsored her in this way.

What is particularly good about this is that the director-general has now taken her up as his mentee. In this foreign assignment he has given her considerably autonomy, an enormous opportunity for growth. I have heard from her recently. She is enjoying it greatly.

In this case my sponsorship took the form of explicit advocacy, but it was not as forceful as an instance recounted by Hennig and Jardim. They tell of a mentee who was intended to take over some of her boss's responsibilities, but who felt that the time was not right:

> I was afraid that most male clients were not ready to deal in confidence with a woman. When my boss heard this, he blew his stack. I remember he screamed at me that it was the damnedest time for me to have an identity crisis. What he did was amazing to me then; he went out to see every client we had and told them they would be working with me. He told them that I was the most skilled

and able publicist in the company and they would be damn lucky if their account happened to be placed in my charge. Before I knew what was happening, our clients were actually asking for me, and I was getting more accounts than I and my group could handle . . . (p132).

Political Knowledge and Access to the Informal Network

Mentors are vital in explaining how a company functions not only in mechanical terms, but also what the political structures are, and this is perhaps the most important benefit they can provide for a mentee wanting to get on, for without political nous people certainly cannot get far. One respondent talked of learning how to get things done, rather than what the official channels were that people were meant to go through. Another said her mentor gave her 'an appreciation of strategy, explaining organisational quirks, *modus operandi*, politics, making one streetwise,' so that she 'learned how to put your organisation in context and *manage* it, and even more important *change* it with people's cooperation and enthusiasm.'

You cannot do these things unless you are part of the informal network of an organisation. It could take you years to find out how informal information – gossip, the latest company news, who's up for promotion, who definitely isn't, where the new subsidiary will be based – is passed. But your mentor can take you straight in, as we saw with the after-hours sports club discussed earlier. As a friend of mine put it, this puts a whole new meaning into the expression 'See you later.' Not an obscene suggestion from the boss, but an invitation to promote your promotion.

Since the importance of joining the sports club is so company specific, this behaviour cannot be transferred wholesale to other organisations. But the learning can. All companies have their informal networks in which those who want promotion (or just gossip) are wise to join. Other organisations network in wine bars, on theatre trips, at company dinners, etc and if you are not around, you miss out. The first my own brother heard of his promotion to head of a large and important department was when the group chairman announced it in his after-dinner speech at the annual dinner, one hundred miles away from the company head-quarters in absolutely foul weather. There is no doubt in my brother's mind that if he had not been seen to be there keeping the side up, he would not have got that promotion.

This question of the informal network cannot be overestimated, nor can the benefit of having a mentor who belongs to the network and can introduce you to it. Recognising the importance of networking with the right people, locating where the power is, and then actually networking with the powerful, is something to which women must give serious attention. People matter, and the way you relate to people with influence is probably the most significant factor in determining which side of the glass ceiling you end up on.

Mentoring Anecdotes

The anecdotes below illustrate some of the things that women have learned or passed on in their mentoring experience.

Don't Copy Blindly
It can be disastrous if you blindly incorporate features into your own behaviour which you have learned elsewhere, but which really do not sit well with your personality. Gail was already mature and had run her own private accountancy practice for some years when she decided she wanted to enter corporate management. Having been taken on by a large retail chain, she was participating in their trainee scheme for senior managers, shadowing the general manager of one of the chain's northern outlets. This man was a good mentor to her, and explained the thinking behind his various actions. He explained the need to be ruthless and get the people you wanted on your team, and exemplified this by telling how he had pinched the display manager from a competitor. When she, in turn, had her own branch she remembered this reasoning and pinched the member of her mentor's very own display team that she wanted on her team. But she had to give him back! The northern manager made a big fuss and she didn't have the stomach for that sort of behaviour.

Gail uses this experience in mentoring others. She recognises in retrospect that this had been naïve on her part. She had followed blindly a stratagem which she personally found distasteful, but had done it because she thought this was what the company expected of her. What she did not realise was that to do this and keep the person concerned she had to be not only ruthless and consistent in her ruthlessness, but she also had to be convinced in her own personality and her own morality that this behaviour was right for her. She was not. This was not her management style. So that episode was a sad but salutary lesson.

Same Effect, Different Strategy

Sometimes you know what you want to achieve, but you find that the way other people achieve this does not appeal to you. You have to find other ways of doing the same thing. One mentor tells the story of a woman who was the only female in a particular work team. The whole team, boss and peer colleagues, regularly went off to the pub at lunch time. Like many women, this woman did not like drinking at lunch time, nor did she like the smoke, the noise and the general atmosphere. And although she made an effort to overcome her dislike and occasionally went with them, she did not go regularly. Unfortunately, this was interpreted as her being too 'snobby' to drink with the boys. In fact, she was very miserable because this left her out in the cold. She realised that this was one of their ways of staying close as a group and having informal discussions about work, contacts, etc.

She was worried that she was missing out and feared for her own development and promotion. She sought advice from her mentor. Her advice was to give a barbecue and invite her colleagues round to show that she was not too snobby to mix with them in a social situation. The evening turned out to be a great success, thanks largely to her dog! She discovered that her boss also had a dog that he was very fond of, and this established a point of (human) contact that they had not had before. After this, although she still did not enjoy the pub, she and her boss, through their shared interest in dogs, were able to keep in informal contact so that she did not miss out on the networking that went on in the pub.

Getting the Intended Message Across

The question of how women appear to think, because of the language they use in expressing their thoughts, is vitally important. Last year I was at a conference in Cambridge University where all the participants were women academics or senior university administrators. After one discussion paper had been read nineteen of the women present made responses. Of those nineteen, twelve started their comments with 'I'd just like to say . . .' In one sense, they are being inefficient, taking up time with a preamble which added nothing to their point. They also, and perhaps this is even worse in general terms, appeared to be discounting the value of what they were about to say. It was as if they were saying 'Forgive me for opening my mouth and taking up your time. Really I've got nothing important to say.' To which any sane person with work to do wants to say, 'Then sit down and let us get on with things.'

This introduction to a point is very common in women. It stems from three things: our low self-esteem, which we express in learned speech habits, even in front of other women; our traditional upbringing as compassionate carers in society; and our later failure to recognise that in the workplace this may not be our primary role. Such an introduction to a remark can be quite legitimately used to ease your way into a difficult situation, where caution is called for: 'I don't want you to be hurt by this remark, it's a small point, but I'd really just like to say that that colour doesn't do anything for your complexion.' The intellectual part of the message is 'don't wear that colour.' The whole of the preamble relates to the relationship between the speaker and the person being addressed.

But this expression can also be used strategically. Using it can be a clever way of making sure that people hear your voice and stop talking in time for you to make your important point. A mentor can be very helpful in helping you to improve the way you express yourself so that your way of talking gives a positive image of your thoughts.

Use All Available Resources, Fully

During an inspection visit a main-board director had praised one woman for the particular project she had been leading and seemed generally pleased with her work. Then he asked to speak to her in private. She was quite alarmed when he began to talk about her use of her expense account, fearing that she had unwittingly abused it in some way. He asked, 'Now, what do you think we gave it to you for?' She recalls mumbling something about using it to entertain people, the press, buyers, etc. to advertise her products. He then startled her by asking, 'But have you been doing it?' She hadn't been using it *enough*!

In her attempts not to waste the money, to use it wisely, she had hardly used it at all. Her sense of thrift had been quite misplaced. What she regarded as a way of retaining money for the company, he regarded as a way of failing to make more money for the company. He ended the conversation with a lesson she has learned to apply elsewhere: 'This sort of thing requires investment. Always make sure you use a resource when it is given to you.'

Asking for Help

One of the things that women consistently fail to do is ask for what they want. They wait around expecting the world to be fair, anticipating that it will be their turn next for an equitable distribution of the goodies. It rarely is. At best they feel unlucky, at worst they feel victimised and unfairly treated. These things can be true, but women can learn to help themselves by rejecting the traditional conditioning that stops them from putting themselves forward, and instead saying what they want. The following story shows a woman failing to ask for what she desperately needs, advice.

Willa had come to live in Britain a few years earlier and was trying to re-establish her career as a freelance interior designer. She was having difficulty getting work. We were talking about the people she could reach through her various networks, which were already fairly well-established at a social level. It transpired that the husband of one of the mums she met regularly at the school her children went to was an architect. Had she contacted him for advice, I asked. She seemed pretty shocked at the suggestion. Why should he help her? He hardly knew her. To which my reply was that if she didn't ask him, he certainly couldn't help her. Would a man have hesitated?

Making Requests

In making requests for things, you not only stand a chance of getting what you ask for, but you also make yourself more visible than if you just sit back and wait for things to happen to you. If you couple visibility with personal credibility you could be on to a winner. Paula was very worried when a particularly interesting project, which had involved new areas of responsibility, came to an end, for the work on the horizon seemed pretty bleak and unexciting. She had not yet learned that few chances for greater responsibility fall in your lap. You have to seek them out. You have to show desire and preparedness for more responsibility and for promotion. And you have to say clearly, if not exactly bluntly, that you are ready to move on.

> My mentor said I should go to my line manager and say how much I had enjoyed that project, and the chance to develop new skills. She also advised me to ask if there were any more similar projects in the pipeline. It worked. I was given a rise in salary and a place on the next project team within a couple of months.

Handling Meetings

Personal visibility can also be increased at meetings. You have to learn to speak up. Not so long ago I was at a public lecture where the speaker was an eminent European Parliamentarian talking on opportunities for business in Europe in 1992. The audience was packed with senior people, mostly men, all middle-aged, grey-haired and grey-suited, from the business world. But the first person to ask a question after the talk was a young woman, 32 years old as it later transpired. This made quite an impression. It had been calculated: 'Just before I left, my boss said to me, "Say something. It doesn't matter what you say, but make sure people notice you. And always start by giving your name, job and company." '

I wouldn't accept this advice wholesale. I think it does matter what you say. But the rest I accept. Being visible, being known, is important. If people don't see you, they don't know you exist. So how can they take an interest in you or promote you?

I remember an exasperating occasion when I was chairing a meeting of several hundred delegates to a national conference. Two women indicated to me beforehand that they wished to speak. Ever interested in playing my part in affirmative action, I turned to them frequently during the debate, but never did they stick up a hand to catch my eye. At the end of the discussion I asked them, with a certain edge to my voice, why they had changed their mind. Both said that previous speakers had made the point they wanted to make, so they hadn't bothered.

I wanted to bang their heads together. Who will the influential people in the room remember, those who spoke, or those who remained silent? There are times for silence, but a national meeting is not one of them. There was no reason in the world why they could not have stood up and said, 'Madam Chair, I am happy to reinforce the point just made by Bill Bloggs. The kind of

behaviour that he mentioned is typical of our region where . . .'
They would have reinforced a good point and drawn positive
attention to themselves, as well as adding new evidence to the
debate. But they were women. And women remain silent in a
mixed public meeting unless there is a reason not to. Speak up
ladies. There is nothing to fear but your promotion.

Dressing Appropriately

If clothes maketh man, they certainly maketh woman. Because
women are still so rare in business or in public positions of
responsibility they are (ironically) highly visible, and the clothes
they wear, the visual signals they send out about themselves, are
particularly noticeable. And clothes, of course, are only one
outward symbol of what groups we belong to, or want to belong
to. Our cars, our homes, even the way we dress our children, all
say something about us, offer other people clues in judging us. In
some situations in life we have a free hand about what to wear.
Not in business. Whether we like it or not, whether it is playing
silly games or not, the way we look and the clothes we wear matter
to our acceptance in a given job, and a given company. They are a
major factor in determining recruitment and promotion.

Because there are so few women in the business world, junior
women have few role models to give them guidance, conscious or
unconscious, in their dress, so women are overtly conscious of
their visual image and are now turning to that new breed of
adviser, image consultants, to help them with their dress at work.
They pay large sums of money to be advised, or even have their
wardrobes dictated, by these consultants. Image consultants
advise men too, particularly those who are otherwise successful,
but who do not 'visually fit' the next rung up the ladder. In com-
parison few men engage their services, since men usually have
enough role models to emulate. So it was particularly interesting
to watch the race to the image consultants when permission was
eventually given for the proceedings of the House of Commons to
be televised!

There are courses and seminars, often run by women's professional associations, that you can attend on business dressing,
authority dressing, power dressing, call it what you will, and there
are books that you can read. Take these with a goodly handful of
salt, and don't dress outside your own comfort level, but always

remember that a man doesn't stay on the cricket team long if he doesn't wear whites.

Sheila Needham says that her male boss/mentor taught her 'the importance of looking smart and successful'. She certainly took that lesson to heart. She also says that when she meets people who have heard of her but never before met her, they sometimes say that they are surprised by how feminine she looks. When you are the owner of a multi-million-pound printing business you can choose how feminine you want to look. Until then, find out what the company form is and accept it. Follow your mentor's lead.

Even Anita Roddick, entrepreneur of Body Shop fame, had to conform in the beginning. She recounts the numerous times she tried to raise money to start her now world-famous business, only to be turned down time and again. Until she got the message that she had to wear a business suit when visiting a bank manager and playing the role of successful entrepreneur in the making.

Advice with dressing is important for women returners. They often do not know current trends or standards. I once even had to tell a woman returning in her late thirties, that turning her skirt hem up with long running stitches in contrasting thread was not appropriate. She, like many other women, spent so much time and effort turning her husband and children out well that she had stopped doing it for herself. But she was now back in the world of business and domestic habits would not do.

Communication Skills

Most women with whom I have discussed mentoring have talked about the importance of developing good communication skills. Good communication depends not only on being in contact, but being in the kind of contact you actually want to be in. It depends on being very clear about the messages you are sending out about yourself, and making sure that the messages other people are receiving are those that you are wanting to send. I remember once advising someone not to apply to a City accountancy firm on puce-coloured paper. Her explanation was that it would stick in the mind of the recruiter. I accepted this, but said that the message the recruiter received would be the negative one of non-conformity, casualness, arrogance and lack of suitability, rather than the posi-tive one of creativity and enterprise she wanted to communicate. She later went into advertising.

Communication covers a whole range of issues, but here I want specifically to look at language, both speech and body language.

Speech Someone who has been mentoring women for years always alerts her clients to the importance of choosing their words carefully, and she recounts a story from her own experience. Fairly early on in her career she was asked by a colleague: 'Now tell me, how do you see your future?' She replied: 'I'd like to run my own department one day.' To her this was an honest reply, stating her dream and implying her belief in herself. It was however interpreted by malicious gossipers as an admission that she was after her boss's job. This went around, and got back to her. She was very worried, because she respected her boss and did not want to have any misunderstanding. Although very concerned about this she did not rush to him and explain, but waited a while and mentioned it quietly to him at a later date. He said yes, he had heard the rumour too, but had taken no notice of it. He had assumed it was malicious gossip.

She was fortunate to have such a sensible boss. But she could have been more careful about the language she had chosen. If she had completed her brief statement with 'when the time is right' or 'when I've got sufficient experience', or even just included a word like 'eventually' or 'ultimately', her sentence would have been less open to the interpretation it was given. You cannot legislate for malice, but you can develop an awareness to the language you are using and the possible (mis)interpretation it is open to.

Body Language I have recently had a slightly difficult scene with someone in a group discussion. There were eleven of us (all women) sitting around a large round table listening to each person speak in turn about the development of her own business. Every woman except one was leaning forward looking at the person speaking, giving the impression of engaged interest. The remaining one was leaning back in her chair, not looking at the speaker and not appearing to be interested in what was going on. Part of my function that day was to help these new business women improve their communication with clients, so I asked this one person if she didn't see the relevance of what the others were saying to her own situation. She was startled at the suggestion, and asked what made me ask that. I explained that her body language,

101

her position and her eye movements, were sending me that message. She was indignant and became quite defensive, telling me that my interpretation was quite wrong (I think she said that *I* was wrong, not my *interpretation*): she was most certainly listening, she was giving the impression of being relaxed yet part of the action, she had been told that leaning forward was a sign of aggression, etc.

I began to regret having made the observation. It took me a long time to get her to understand that the signals she intended to transmit were very different from the signals that I (and every other group member) was receiving. It was particularly unfortunate for her since she had done some reading in body language, and was trying to put her reading into practice. But she had failed to understand that a combination of factors is important. She was acting on the belief that leaning back means relaxed encouragement, and leaning forward aggression. Certainly these positions can mean that, but whether they do depends also on the kind of chair you are sitting in, what you are doing with your head, hands, eyes, whether you are smiling, etc. She just got the combination wrong.

Body language is very important. Men learn about the kind of body language required in a work situation because they are surrounded by role-models, 'working fathers' at home, businessmen on television, men in the workplace, etc. Most women do not have other women as role models. They rarely have suitable role models in the home unless their mother has herself been in business or had a voluntary management role in a charity. Senior businesswomen at work are still few and far between, and even when they are portrayed on television or in the media generally they are usually so caricatured as to be unsuitable as role models. Women mentors are very important in this respect. And women's networks can also provide aspiring women with role models to follow. Not only do they bring together like-minded women, for emulation as it were, but they also run courses to make women overtly aware of body language. There are also a number of books on the subject.

Lone Woman

The isolation of the sole woman in the team or in the company can be pretty hard to bear. Even when there is no apparent sex bias in the operational work of an organisation, there are all sorts of fringe behaviours and needs in all organisations that make a sole woman feel very isolated. (Like lack of loos, to put it at its most basic.) Being isolated is bad enough, but actually being *excluded* from things just because you are a woman is scandalous if not, in the following instance, unlawful. Virginia Novarra relates the following almost unbelievable story. She had been working for about fourteen years and had not been aware of discrimination. She was now the only woman among a small executive group in her department and one Christmas

> was told without ceremony by my senior colleagues that it would not be possible for me to attend the Christmas lunch for the senior staff, or a lunch given for them by a principal client organization, because the first of these functions was traditionally held in an all-male professional club, and the second in an all-male senior executives' mess (p13).

At least if she had had a mentor, someone who had a serious belief in her abilities, she would have had someone to take her anger seriously, someone who understood the barbarity of what her colleagues had just done to her, and who could have stood with her in her battle against injustice. Her colleagues didn't.

Problems

Notwithstanding all the benefits that being mentored can bring, a small minority of women have encountered some difficulties. These are described here, not to stop you from seeking mentoring, but to alert you to potential problems that you should watch out for. These mostly relate to women mentees in cross-gender mentoring.

Sexual Connotations
Some firms do not tolerate any form of sexual partnership at work, and even when couples announce their intention to become engaged or they marry, one partner is obliged to leave the firm, or move to another department. This of course affects the promotion prospects for one or other of the partners.

Even where a firm has no such policy, sexual attraction can still

103

have its problems, and the nature of the mentoring relationship between a senior man and a junior woman can give rise to particular difficulties. In this relationship the male has power over the female, both in the best sense of being able to help her, and in the worst of being able unfairly to manipulate her.

A mentor is always by definition someone who has achieved a degree of success, and this is a powerful sexual attractant. It is particularly attractive to young women starting out on their careers, or to older women who do not have a regular sexual relationship or whose arrangements are no longer exciting. I have therefore to say to you, as I would to any of my mentees, that you should think very carefully about embarking on a sexual relationship with your mentor. I am not saying don't. I do, after all, know of several good marriages where the husband was originally the wife's mentor. (And two well-known 'mentoring' marriages are those of Elisabeth Schwarzkopf and Walter Legge, and Dame Joan Sutherland and Richard Bonynge.) But I am saying think twice, for men who are thwarted in their sexual endeavours can be very nasty creatures, and mentors who are thwarted are in positions of power which make them particularly dangerous.

Refusing to respond to a mentor's sexual advances does not always lead to disaster. Sheila Needham admits that there was some degree of sexual attraction between herself and her mentor, but she was determined this would not develop. This caused a degree of coolness on the part of her mentor, but they continued working together. And another of my respondents said 'There was a sexual attraction which I didn't return, but he was never unfair or manipulative about it.'

Unfortunately things are not always that civilised. The worst thwarted-mentor case I ever had to deal with involved rape. The young woman concerned had admittedly been very attracted to her mentor, a successful, internationally recognised authority in his field, also her head of department, and married. Early in their relationship she had had a sexual relationship with him. But he would not accept her change of heart, and threatened her not only with a bad annual assessment, but disclosure of the worst kind. Her continued refusal to consent to his continued advances merely enraged him and one day, finding her not at work, and learning that she was at home ill, he let himself into her flat with the key he still had and raped her, repeating his threats of disclosure if she reported him. Appalling enough though this was, it was further complicated by the fact that she could not easily leave the company because she was foreign and working under a restrictive work permit. Fortunately she had the sense to tell me. I believed her. I consulted the director of personnel, a man in whose judgement and discretion I trusted, and he also believed her.

Sexual harassment at work is now taken seriously, and there are legal remedies. But they are not pain-free, and can have catastrophic consequences for the individuals and their families. We therefore did not resort to law. Between us we resolved the situation discreetly. But we used utterly unorthodox methods, and both people eventually left, one fortunately with a future still ahead of her, and the other with that bit of his past definitely behind him.

I know of another situation in which a woman left her job because of her male mentor. He became very possessive of her, and his constant attention caused his wife to be resentful and jealous. This, coupled with his mentee's growing assertiveness and refusal to allow him too much control of her life, eventually led to his breakdown, and her departure.

But sex-related problems arise even in honourable situations. On one occasion I had to make sure that annual performance assessments for a junior female were obtained from several people, not just her official assessor. Not because he was dishonourable, but precisely the opposite. The two people concerned were engaged to be married, quite openly, and neither of them thought the assessment would be a problem, because they both believed he could be objective. But nobody else did. They thought he would mark her down! So other people had to be involved.

In the situation above the comments of other people were positive, but this is not always the case. Even the threat of gossip, misunderstanding and unpleasantness can jeopardise a mentoring relationship. For this often involves spending time together at work and elsewhere, like restaurants, hotels, conferences, at home and abroad. You may have to put up with some negative reaction, particularly if your mentor is an older man. You might not like it, and although I am not aware that this has ever caused problems to my male colleagues, Odiorne in particular has noted that some men are uncomfortable about it. He reports one man as saying, 'I don't like one damn bit the prospect of facing a lot of cheap leers and sly remarks, even if they were totally unfounded or were only being done in a jovial way.'

This is a rotten comment on our society, and I hope that increasing numbers of women in the workplace will soon make such sentiments less frequent.

But gossip is nevertheless a problem, and some men react by trying to get out of mentoring women. This is tough on the women if there are no women suitable to be mentors in the company. If this is the case for you, then you must seek mentoring relationships (with men or women) in your other networks.

Other men for whom gossip is a threat will accept female mentees, but they restrict the breadth and nature of their activities, not doing anything with them that could give rise to suspicion. If this is a problem in your mentoring relationship you must be extra vigilant and take steps to see that you don't miss out on anything vital. Make sure that you still get the same share of special attention, private meetings, etc. that male mentees would get. So make a particular effort to suggest meetings in a controlled environment, where you can have a private conversation but without intimate surroundings, in a staff canteen, for example, or in your respective offices where you can both be seen.

And if you are not being taken to conferences, etc. with your mentor because of overnighting in hotels, then try and go with a female colleague, or on your own.

There are yet other cross-gender problems for women mentees which, whilst not being overtly sexual, clearly have a sexual connotation. One women says 'My mentor showed an unhealthy and uncalled-for interest in my domestic arrangements and often made moral judgements. Also I was cautioned for being too messy and told to take more care with my appearance.' Up to this point it is possible to exercise compassion and claim that the man was only being clumsy. But the next statement clinches it. 'He told me to use my femininity and exploit it, wear more make-up and seamed stockings'! Fortunately this particular woman is fairly robust and was able to put up with this kind of rubbish for she was able to learn valuable lessons in networking from her mentor. But in many cases what she learned from him was how *not* to go about things.

Father Figures

Problems can also arise when male mentors behave or act like fathers, even well-meaning ones. Your mentor might well be old enough to be your father, and may in many respects treat you as his daughter, wanting to help you in the same way he would help her. But he might carry this a bit far and enquire into aspects of your life that a father would find appropriate, like domestic and boyfriend arrangements. If you are happy discussing these things, fine. But they are basically none of the mentor's business unless they are causing problems at work, and if you don't want to discuss them you do not have to.

Try and be clear why your mentor is asking these questions before you decide how to handle this. If he has inadvertently got his roles confused, then try to answer very briefly or non-committally. Or look surprised and ask him to repeat the question. If he has to do this, he may realise what he is doing, apologise and be more careful the next time. If you decide he is probing deliberately and unnecessarily, then you could try humour. Try laughing and saying 'Tom, I know you're concerned, but really you don't need to be. I'm a big girl now. I left home long ago!' And if he still persists you will have to be more direct, and say 'Tom, thank you for your concern, but I really don't want to talk about that' and immediately move on to something else, like: 'But I would be glad if we could discuss the paper I've got to present next week.' In this way you hope still to retain his services as a useful adviser, while keeping your private life to yourself.

There is another problem associated with mentor fathers. It is their body language. Real fathers have society's permission to touch their daughter in a way that no mentor may normally touch his mentee. A father, seeing his daughter working late, may well put his hands on her shoulders and give her a squeeze, may even bend to kiss her head, as he leaves her to it, encouraging her, but also giving her a word of advice, saying 'Don't stay up too late.'

Depending on your relationship with your mentor, you may be prepared to accept this as he comes to say goodbye at the end of the day. I can think of some male colleagues from whom I would have accepted something similar (but not mentees!). But in general I would reckon that you have to be careful about this degree of intimacy, in case it gets out of hand. What we have just witnessed above is a man-to-woman scene. It is not a colleague-to-colleague event. What you want is to be taken seriously as a colleague by everyone in your world of work, so don't jeopardise your chances. Don't be stand off-ish, but be careful.

If all else fails leave lying around your office a copy of Kathryn Stechert's book *The Credibility Gap*. She has some useful things to say about body language and the world of work. It can produce some interesting reactions.

Differences Between the Sexes

A further problem concerns the fact that it is impossible for men to understand what it is like to be a woman, brought up in a female culture and now trying to operate in the world of work, largely a male culture. Many, many men do their level best to help women, but they cannot empathise with them, so cannot be helpful in all situations. This can be a problem at a psychological and tactical level. For example, when a woman talks to her mentor about people not taking any notice of her at meetings, he may put the problem down to her quiet voice and suggest that she should speak louder. What she really needs, though, is lessons in being assertive in a male culture.

Being used to the male culture, he doesn't immediately recognise that men and women behave differently in meetings, and cannot understand why she finds it difficult just to bellow until someone listens to her. Nor can he understand that the reaction of her colleagues to her bellowing will be very different, and much less positive, then when he bellows. (This is not always the case: I know at least one woman who can down the opposition at a hundred paces by shouting, but you have to calculate very finely the circumstances in which you do this.) For this sort of cultural problem you just have to talk to a woman who may not have the same problem, but who can 'feel' the nature of yours because of your shared experiences.

In another case a woman doing a management research project found her male mentor 'brilliant' at helping her to analyse the actual subject matter, but he was completely unable to help her to go about the research. She deliberately turned to another woman for this, for she felt that this was a cultural weakness on her part, rather than an intellectual one. She rightly thought that the research method her mentor assumed her to be familiar with revealed a very masculine way of going about things, rather than the more people-orientated method she was initially more comfortable with. The woman academic to whom she turned helped her, without discounting her traditional skills, to add new methods to her research techniques, in order to reach the results they all wanted.

There are other practical consequences of this difference in culture. Male mentors often invite their mentees to the pub at lunch time or after work for a chat in relaxing circumstances, to review progress and to plan for the next stage. But many women, as already discussed, find pubs too noisy, dirty or smoky and would prefer not to go there. And when we suggest this to men they are perplexed. The pub meets their requirements for a relaxed chat, why should it not meet ours? The difficulty here is that if you refuse to go to the pub you miss out on the networking that happens there as well as the private chat with your mentor. So you must find a solution which enables you still to benefit from all aspects of mentoring without having to pay too high a price. Try going to the pub every so often, but also suggest meeting in quieter surroundings on the odd occasion too (see also 'Same Effect, Different Strategy' on p95).

Male Chauvinism?

There are other problems with being mentored by men that women have reported, like having their progress hampered, having too much protection, and having their mentors become dependent on them. In the absence of other evidence, this points to the conclusion that these men were manifesting continuing underlying stereotypical behaviour towards women: they gave them the amount of freedom it suited them to give, but they couldn't give the amount of freedom the women wanted. Interesting.

It is a sad fact of life that some mentors, mercifully a minority, get so attached to their mentees that they are unable to let them get beyond the mentee stage.

> As I grew and developed, I sometimes thought he was holding me back. He decided early on that I would reach a certain ceiling in the structure of the organisation. I decided to prove him wrong (Clutterbuck and Devine, 'Having a Mentor; a Help or a Hindrance?', p98).

One of my own colleagues talks of her mentor's refusal to acknowledge that she was ready 'to go on and up, beyond his control'. And Sheila Needham found that the situation with her mentor became intolerable 'because having encouraged me to grow, he did not want me to build on the confidence he had helped me to develop.' In her case, her mentor could not let her make her own decisions. In the end she left in frustration.

Whilst having protection from your mentor can be very valuable, in certain situations it can prevent you from learning as fast as you would if you had to feel the full force of your errors or misjudgements. As one woman said:

> Rather than letting or helping me to work things out for myself he was often too much of a 'Captain Fixit', meaning well, but too directive and not helping me to develop.

Women mentors seem to be able to let their mentees get their fingers burned, as they do with their children when they persistently play with fire.

I have come across several examples of mentors who are unable to take the final step that will release their mentees, relying strongly on their continuing loyalty. Sheila Needham experienced just this situation:

> When he offered me the job of running the printers (at a time when it had sixteen staff and I was trying to do that job as well as my secretarial duties) he took nearly a year to appoint a new secretary (interviewing *lots* of very suitable girls but not wishing me to go to the new job full time).

I have had a very similar case reported to me. In this instance the woman concerned had been her mentor's personal assistant rather than his secretary, and he had, up to then, treated her very decently, putting her name as well as his on papers that she had helped him with (unheard of in that company). But he could not bear to lose her. He had never had success with secretaries before and took an inordinate time finding a new one. In the end his mentee left before he found her replacement for she had a place to take up at university. The last she heard he was still getting through several secretaries in a year. He had not been able to find a substitute. And in yet another case, the female mentee had to go through a role reversal, becoming her mentor's mentor, so dependent had he become.

We are not talking about love in any of these cases, just dependence. A fundamental need for continuing service. Be prepared! If similar things are happening in your life, despite your mentor's feelings, you must use your wings to fly free. Otherwise it isn't fair. The role of a mentor is to help, not to trap you.

Fortunately the problems reported here are rare. I have included them to alert you to things that can go wrong so that you will be sensitive to difficulties and take whatever evasive action you can at the earliest reasonable stage.

Sheila Needham

Not many people move from being a secretary to owning a printing company with a multi-million-pound turnover. Sheila Needham did. And she acknowledges that this is in large part due to the encouragement she received from an early boss. She says 'My mentor believed I could do things I didn't think I could do, like research in building contract procedures in a country where I didn't speak the language.' He was also something of a stickler for accuracy first time round, and used to hold up her finished letters to the light to see how many mistakes she had corrected with Tippex!

But he had far more confidence in her potential than she did. She often felt thrown in at the deep end when her boss/mentor made demands on her which she didn't feel she could meet. But she survived and thrived. Her big break came when her mentor offered her the chance to become acting MD of a printing company which he had set up, with her help. She accepted, much to his annoyance, because he really wanted her to go on being his secretary! He had come to be very dependent on her. She tried to do both jobs, but eventually found his demands too much, especially when he wanted her to do the payroll when she was in hospital with meningitis!

So armed with the *confidence* she had gained under his

111

mentorship she left to set up her own printing business. And armed with the *skills* she had learned from him she raised the money she needed to do things as she wanted to, as her own boss. She had also helped her mentor do the company entertaining, and learned a lot about how to create a confident company image.

But she never poached clients from him. That was against her ethical principles. And today Sheila continues to preach the need for ethically acceptable conduct in business. She is also very generous to anyone seeking help and advice, and gives much valued support to organisations which help women to develop their potential, as she was able to do with the help of her mentor.

CHAPTER 5

Becoming a Mentor

As I stated earlier, one of the main reasons for writing this book was to help compensate for the failure of our society to give adequate encouragement and support to women in developing their potential to the full, particularly in the world of paid work. In this chapter I appeal directly to those of you in a position to offer mentoring to younger women to consider whether you can help in this way. This means considering your own skills, experience and goals, to see whether mentoring fits in with what you can offer, and what you want to achieve in life. It also means looking around you to see if, in your organisation or other areas where you might have influence, there are women who could benefit from your experience and perspective.

Some people may be puzzled by this plea, for it may seem to be unnecessary: more and more women are undeniably coming into the workplace and entering an ever-increasing number of job areas. But there is no evidence to show that their rise to senior levels is keeping pace with the rate of increase in the numbers of working women.

The reasons for this are many and complex, but I believe one reason to be a touch of naïveness, even complacent naïveness, on the part of some senior people who assume that the mere presence of women in the workforce guarantees women the same level of development opportunities as men. They are very proud to tell me that their company treats women and men exactly the same, and are utterly taken about when I say, 'Why? Women aren't the same as men.' I am, of course, not objecting to their desire to promote women to senior responsibility with the same status and power as men. What I am saying is that women come to the workplace with different 'cultural baggage', a different history and a different set of expectations, and respond to different forms of training and encouragement from those traditionally used for men. And that, therefore, those people responsible for training women to be of maximum value to their company are failing in their duty if they don't take this into account. They know how they themselves have achieved success, or how their colleagues have risen through the ranks, so in their search for others to follow in their footsteps they look for people who demonstrate the same qualities.

For the most part these successful people are men, and searching only in their own image, they find only men to follow on after them. They overlook women, for women are not the same as men, and don't fit the criteria specified. At best, according to this 'sameness' theory they are flawed men, and being flawed they are not suitable for career grooming, What is at fault is not the women, but the criteria of measurement. Women behave differently from men, have different values, are probably more collaborative, less confrontational, more nurturing and caring, and are of considerable value to their company, but not in the same way as men.

For the same reason I am also worried about people who think they are doing a great job when they help women to reach their 'comfort zone'. Despite the fact that I know better, I still interpret this as an American euphemism for the ladies' loo. But that is not my objection. What bothers me is that the term implies a belief that women cannot go further than the level at which they feel comfortable. Acting on this belief merely reinforces the low self-image of women that is evident when they fail to apply for a job because of the high salary offered, despite a job description that falls well within their proven competence. Women as a group have little experience of high salaries, and are therefore uncomfortable with them, so do not apply.

So I want as mentors the kind of people who, knowing that women have been conditioned to expect their achievement to be lower rather than higher, knowing that women are not used to being urged to go that little bit further, will consciously and actively challenge their mentees to go *beyond* their comfort zone, will help them always to strive towards new goals, so that they have an opportunity of achieving more than they originally thought possible. And it is pointless to object, 'You can take a horse to water . . .' We all know that that is true. But if you never even point the horse in the direction of the water, what chance has the poor creature got?

That puts a special burden on us as women. I am asking you, as women already at the top or on your way up, to play your part in making sure that young women get a fair crack of the whip. You may have got there yourself, or claim you have, by your own unaided efforts, but that is not the point. If you believe that women have something to offer the nation other than changing its nappies, and/or you believe that women have a right to the kind of support that successful men often give other men in advancing their career, then please join those of us who want to give other women a hand up the ladder. Become a mentor.

This is not to suggest that you should not mentor young men. Nor is it a plea to promote the unworthy. It is a request that you do two things: that you consciously and actively scrutinise the young women around you to assess their potential for development with your help; and that at the same time you open your mind to signs of talent that may be different from or less evident than those exhibited in young men.

In other words, please start looking under the bushels to see if there are any Christmas roses lurking underneath which you wouldn't have seen if you'd not stooped down to their level. Staying with the horticultural metaphor, let us listen to a senior executive who was talent-spotted while still an apparently unlikely young employee by a sharp-eyed mentor: 'The things I'm getting into now I always had in me, but I needed someone to plant the seed, because I had fertile ground to grow it in' (Zey, p68). That's what I want you, as potential mentors, to do for women.

A Typical Mentoring Relationship

A number of years ago I acted as a trainer on a residential weekend course. Trainers and trainees took their meals together at long trestle tables and I found myself sitting opposite someone wearing the usual assortment of clothes that students choose both to show their independence and because they can't afford anything else. She could have been my daughter. In the conversation common in such gatherings, revolving around the question of what had brought us to that particular course, she showed a certain passion about the status of women. She had left school at the earliest opportunity and gained a qualification which she subsequently realised did little to reveal her capabilities. I remember the moment at which things clicked. Her mouth was saying that she really wanted to get a degree, but her eyes were saying that it was too late and that there was no possible chance. I looked her very firmly in the eyes and said simply 'What's stopping you?' She has recently confirmed that that was the signal she had been waiting for. My brief contact with her was enough to allow me to assess her ability, and my direct question told her that her problems in getting a degree were purely mechanical.

I gave her my card, but did not hear from her. I did not pursue the matter, knowing that if I had anything serious to offer she would contact me. I bumped into her again a couple of months later at a similar course. This time she was helping with the arrangements. I needed some water to drink and she personally took me along to the kitchens and drew my water for me, rather than just showing me where the kitchens were. It was there that we began to talk. And we have talked on and off for several years.

I did not change her life-style. Nor did I choose her degree course, cope with an unplanned pregnancy, or switch her educational establishment and alter her domestic arrangements so that she could properly adjust to the baby. Nor did I make the decision that she should apply for a full-time job and continue her study in the evening. She did all that herself. But I have over the years been available to her when she has needed me.

On the training courses at which we have continued to meet I have made a point of bringing particularly significant things specifically to her attention, and on important social occasions I have commented on her dress and her behaviour. We have had long conversations about her past and her future, and I have held her close when the going has temporarily been too tough. I have occasionally employed her to work for me, and have allowed her to give me as a referee. She knows she can talk to me whenever she needs to, and she has also been told in the traditional no uncertain terms that I will never forgive her if she doesn't get her degree. She knows the real truth of that, but the threat is quite potent.

I have quoted the story above in detail for it demonstrates a 'typical mentoring relationship' measured by a number of factors: we have both benefitted in many of the ways described in preceding chapters; it is based on mutual admiration and mutual respect; we have shared confidences; we have shared tactics and information; we have been together for a number of years. But it is not based in any one organisation, as so many of the relationships quoted in the mentoring literature are. It shows that mentoring can be initiated and maintained outside the workplace, without recourse to formal structures, but still with beneficial effect for mentor and mentee.

Are You Mentor Material?

There are certainly people who have no capacity to mentor others. Those for example who are too busy working on their own tasks, or sorting out their own future, to be interested in encouraging the development of younger people. And also those who claim that they have made it on their own and feel everyone else should too. This does not, of course, prevent younger people from admiring certain characteristics of both these categories of people, and deriving benefit from their existence by using them as non-mentoring role-models.

I am assuming, however, that if you have read this far you do not come into either of the categories above, and that you agree in principle with mentoring, but are not sure whether you are the right sort of person to be a mentor. There can be no simple answer to this. My own experience, that of my colleagues and friends, that of the respondents to my survey and the existing literature on mentoring all indicate that there is no classic mentor type. The academic literature makes a distinction between mentors, instructors, coaches (see Megginson), but basically it doesn't matter what you call yourself. What matters is your attitude and how you manifest that attitude. If you want to help women along the road to success, and you are prepared to put some time and effort into this, then you are probably mentor material, and the rest will fall into place with a little help from friends and colleagues in your various networks.

In fact, you may already be acting as a mentor without realising it. People are often taken aback by the gratitude that younger colleagues express about the help that they have given. They usually say with embarrassment that they only chatted to them on occasion, or just gave them a few hints. So it may be the title of 'mentor' that is problematic for you. You may not see yourself as a mentor, but perhaps you do actually offer 'mentoring' in your everyday work without labelling it as such.

Let us take an example of mentoring-type behaviour and see how your behaviour towards younger colleagues matches up to it.

We will assume that you are the head of the membership services division of a large professional association, and that you have a new employee. By way of induction, you could quite simply assign a particular task to her, perhaps processing the details of new members, give her some basic instruction about what to do and leave her to get on with it. This is the minimum that a superior should do. But you go one stage further and tell her that if she has any problems or suggestions she should come to you. If you have gone this far, you have already shown some characteristics of a mentor, for you have acknowledged the possibility of creative imagination in your employee by mentioning that she might have suggestions rather than just problems.

You then explain to her, fairly soon after she starts working for you, how the particular task assigned to her fits in with other aspects of membership records, what details are kept on computer file, what details can be extracted from the computer, how membership characteristics can be used for marketing purposes, what types of marketing increases membership, thus providing more funds for training, research, lobbying Ministers, etc. In this way you are giving her an overview of the workings of the association, allowing her to have her place in it, in this way making her comfortable and allowing a closeness, an allegiance, to the association to grow. This in turn will enable her to make creative suggestions for change about one small area in ways which she can see benefitting the association as a whole.

In addition to creating an environment in which she can be creative and helpful, you have also given her your personal attention. This makes her feel valued. And people who know they are valued work much better for the people who value them.

By saying that she can come to you with problems you have also shown yourself to be a decent human being with qualities of sympathy and understanding. And again you have shown that you value her, for you have expressed a willingness to listen to her problems, presumably with the intention of helping to solve them.

Also by giving her an overview you have shown that you are a person with perspective. To her this means that you can grasp the wider issues, and can view her suggestions and her problems in a wider context. This implies that you can judge her suitability for work in other areas.

Later she comes to you saying that she has to reply to a letter from a member complaining about the new direct-debit system, and an over-payment on the annual subscription. You could simply tell her what to reply, and if time is short you may do this. You could also tell her to ask one of the others to help. But in addition to this you arrange for her to visit the book-keeping section to see just how things are done. You are thus educating her beyond the strict requirements of your own division, and making her more and more flexible in terms of future deployment. You are also, of course, testing the way she behaves in the other department and what their view is of her.

At a certain stage you tell her that you'd like to have a chat over lunch, just to see how things are going. Over lunch you tell her about the conference for members that is being arranged by another section of your division, and sound her out on whether she would be available to help over that particular weekend. You apologise that she has to give up a weekend, but explain that being involved in that particular conference is very important because of the people she will meet, and how influential they can be in deciding where next she will work in the company. You say that it was at one of these conferences that you met Dr Bloggs, and it was through her that you were promoted to your present job, etc.

You are thus demonstrating an interest in her future, showing her the importance of networks, sharing a few details about your own promotional route, helping her to understand the company culture, telling her about assessment and promotion procedures, showing her where the power lies, etc.

None of this is obligatory in the training you give to a new employee, but it is vital to her, and her understanding of her own possible career development. It will help her to clarify whether she can see her future in this organisation, and indeed whether she wants to work for a company that works this way. But if she does want to stay, she has now been alerted to how she must behave if she wants promotion.

She will also learn from this interchange that you have views and visions which go beyond your own division and your own immediate responsibilities, and that in communicating them to her you are connecting with those qualities in her. You have now also revealed to her that you have qualities of aspiration, that you are successful in your aspirations (therefore worth using as a role model), that you are prepared to discuss things with her, that you are a source of wisdom and guidance, that you are prepared to share your knowledge with her, knowledge which, while still being work related, goes beyond the immediate requirements of the work, and can be helpful to her future, etc. You have presented her with an opportunity for wider visibility and exposure. And you have also issued a challenge: you have invited her to prove her mettle.

These are all very basic things, and you may well do most of them fairly regularly in the routine of your work. But they are what makes the difference between mentoring and 'just managing'. This in itself doesn't make a mentoring relationship, but the seed has been sown. Whether or not it develops into a mentoring relationship depends very much on the employee. The offer has been made, and it is up to her to decide whether to accept it. But you will have demonstrated your capacity to be a mentor.

Finding a Mentee

But to be a mentor, you have to have a mentee, and finding one may not be that simple. Even if you already mentor younger men, you cannot mentor a younger woman until you have found a younger woman to mentor. And if younger women are a rarity in your world, then you have to meet them outside the workplace, in your various networks, formal or otherwise. These could include your professional association or trade union, a women's network, a sports club or simply the block of flats in which you live.

Introducing Yourself
Since those of us able to offer mentoring are more experienced in the world of work and usually older than our potential mentees,

the onus is on us to take the initiative and indicate that we are available for mentoring duty. We have to make ourselves and our willingness known. This is fairly easy with women in your own organisation over whom you have some 'legitimate' control. Your readiness to act as a mentor will come out of the kind of behaviour indicated in the last few pages. But it can be tricky actually making contact with other women more distant in your organisation or elsewhere. I work with extremely senior and competent women who would be happy to help younger women but who blench at the thought of approaching them with mentoring in mind. One said to me recently, 'I'm surrounded by men, I'd love to mentor a woman, but I haven't the faintest idea how I'd go about it.' Which is pretty extraordinary, because women are a very friendly lot and have helped each other through the ages.

Again we can attribute this paradox to the changing role of women in society and the adjustment necessary on the part of us all. If we were just all women together there wouldn't be a problem. But in mentoring we are talking about professional status, and that makes life more complicated. Studies of earlier women managers and executives show them throwing the baby out with the bath water, suppressing their 'womanness' because they felt it to be unhelpful or even damaging in a business setting. They even deliberately dressed in dull unfeminine suits. Hennig and Jardim have reported on such behaviour and the unhappiness it caused the women concerned.

Fortunately we are now learning not to compartmentalise: we have understood that you don't stop being a woman just because you are also a highly paid manager, or the owner of your own business. And you don't stop having an affinity with other women merely because there is a hierarchical difference between you, the successful and the wanting-to-be-successful. We know now that we can be successful in business terms and retain our womanness.

And that womanness is precisely what we as potential mentors to other women can use in making contact with them. As women talking to other women about traditionally feminine subjects, like clothes, we can make our existence and our availability known in a non-threatening way. And unless there are clear indications to the contrary, we do have to approach other women in an indirect non-threatening way, for anything more directly to the point could be counterproductive.

Grieve me as it does, we have to recognise that accepting help from other people (which is what networking and mentoring are all about) is still not recognised by women in England as a legitimate route to advancement. Anything too direct can be tricky not only with women of low self-esteem who 'wouldn't want to put you to any trouble', but also with post feminists. Post feminists believe that all the battles are over, so woman-to-woman help may be considered not only unnecessary but positively unwelcome: the offer of such help can be inferred as a statement that you think a junior woman can't manage without you. It is only in formal schemes where potential mentors and mentees are seeking each other that you can say, 'Hi, I'd like to mentor you', without danger of being misunderstood.

To be academic about this, a comment like 'I like the blouse' from one woman to another falls into the category of what sociolinguists call 'phatic communion'. The message you are sending out is nothing really to do with the blouse. The real function of your comment is to open a channel of communication between you. It is a way of saying 'I am a friendly human being, and you can talk to me if you want to without my being offended.' As a race we do this in Britain, to the bemusement of foreigners, by talking about the weather. Woman to woman, to the bemusement of men, we talk about clothes.

Suitable opening gambits can be made in the ladies' loo (see the earlier chapter on networking), in a lift, sitting in a canteen, in the bar at a sports club. I often initiate contact when standing in a queue anywhere there might be women who could do with my help or the help of someone else I could refer her to. 'I couldn't help admiring your suit. Is it French?' for example, allows me to initiate a conversation which can hardly be construed as offensive, and allows me to judge from the response whether the woman concerned is happy to talk to a stranger or not. If she ignores me or just says 'No', then I back off gracefully. But I might try again at a later stage if I have any reason to believe we could be valuable to each other.

Or, if you prefer the 'caring woman' gambit, when you see someone yawning you can always say 'Oh dear. Late night?' And if she grins and replies 'Sorry. Yes. I'm studying for my accountancy exams,' then you know that she is happy to talk and reveal something about herself, and you can follow by showing something in your own life that you have in common: 'I remember when I was doing my last set of exams. There were five in a row and I don't think I slept a wink during the entire week.' This has nothing directly to do with mentoring, but it has a lot to do with revealing yourself as a sympathetic human being with similar experiences prepared to talk and share your experiences. Further contact can come from there.

There may be some people out there who really can't understand why I am going into such detail here. Such people obviously don't need help at this level. But there are a lot who do. For some people I have actually prescribed exercises so that they can approach other women. So used are they to having only men as colleagues that they are unsure how to deal with women.

Formal Introductions

Making our availability known is easier for us if we belong to an organisation where mentoring is encouraged in a formal scheme, and all we have to do is follow the guidelines. Such schemes may be available in training establishments, at the workplace, or in various networks, through competitions or private career development arrangements. The factor which unifies them is their specific intention to bring potential mentors and mentees together. We shall look at these more closely in the chapter on mentoring schemes. For the moment let us assume that we have no problem in getting to know people either formally or casually, so that we can now concentrate on how we choose from amongst our female acquaintances those people who will be our mentees.

Choosing a Mentee

In most of the mentoring situations about which I have knowledge considerable freedom of choice is exercised by the individual. Even if you are constrained by a company scheme to mentor someone who does not meet your ideal criteria, there is nothing to stop you from also choosing someone else inside your company for informal mentoring, or someone quite outside your work situation. Let us assume that you can exercise some choice, and examine in turn the factors which will determine your choice of mentee. This will depend on your personal philosophy, the framework within which you carry out your mentoring, what you each expect of each other, personality factors, etc.

Using Female Values

In preceding paragraphs I have been talking about making contact. I do not want to give the impression that making contact will necessarily lead to a mentoring relationship, let alone a good one. But I am asking you, in my campaign to help women develop to their full potential, to make a point of introducing yourself routinely to younger women who cross your path. I ask this for two reasons: firstly, so that the younger women know that you are there if they need an older woman to turn to; secondly, so that you actively assess the field of young women available to you, so that no one is dismissed as a future leader for want of obvious flair.

As women we owe it to the next generation to assess very carefully whether with our help unpromising cases can be helped to future greatness. Women's behaviour cannot always be assessed correctly by the usual standards found in business or other predominantly male environments. But as women we know the cultural difficulties under which women labour and should be alive to signs that most men cannot see.

For example, someone who says that she does not understand something is not necessarily admitting that she is a fool or that the subject is beyond her. She may just be admitting an ignorance which her male peer may equally possess but does not admit to. In which case it is her political *nous* that requires attention, not her subject knowledge. Or she may be properly assessing her own ability when she says she does not understand, and may be asking for help, for example, to be sent on a course.

She may also, of course, be saying that she doesn't understand, because she has seen a deeper problem than the others are looking at. I know of a case like this which had considerable repercussions.

A group of fairly senior people who needed some financial information were being taken through the end-of-year accounts by the finance officer. When the woman (the only woman present) said she didn't understand they all assumed she meant that she couldn't read a source and applications statement. What she actually meant was that she couldn't understand why a particular set of figures were included under one heading, when to have given them a separate heading would have made the picture much clearer.

Too clear, as it turned out. The powers that be had been hoping not to let those particular items of expenditure become too obvious. But by then it was too late. She earned herself both brownie points and black marks for the bit of stated ignorance, but she did well out of it in the end.

And all sorts of inhibitions develop in women which a touch of loving care can help overcome. One of my most spectacular successes (the credit goes to both of us) was in refusing to drop someone who failed time and again to pass her exams because of exam phobia. Between us, after much intensive work together, we managed to get her into the exam room long enough to prove her ability. Fourteen years younger than I am, she is now earning far more than I and has a much more secure future.

I am not asking you to promote women who do not merit promotion. I am simply asking you to be alert to signs of development potential which a brief glance would allow others to overlook. And of course I am not suggesting that you overlook the usual signs of future potential, like obvious interest, exercise of initiative, quickness of response, understanding of detail and the place of detail in the wider perspective, etc. I just ask you to look for other signs as well.

The Framework of Choice

The framework in which you choose people to mentor must also be considered. If, for example, you mentor someone in your own workplace then political considerations come into play more crucially than if your mentee is outside, for your direct influence over that person's life and development is greater. Inside the company you are likely to have direct influence over the person's training, work schedule, special assignments, promotion, salary, status, etc. So the way you and your mentee fit together in terms of work ability and ambition is vitally important.

There is evidence that mentors who are sufficiently influential to have a fairly free hand deliberately choose as mentees people with skills complementary to their own, or skills that the mentors possess to a lesser degree, so that they can get a better balance of skills on their management team and thus run their unit or division better. I have seen this happen, for example, where the existing head knows that her unit has to get an influx of new technology if it is to retain its productive capacity and contribution to the organisation as a whole. So she chose someone who had newly acquired and highly developed computer skills.

Other people deliberately choose mentees with marketing or research skills, and together mentor and mentee run the show better. There is nothing new about this phenomenon as such. It is seen all the time in job advertisements, where specific characteristics are singled out for special mention in order to boost a department's strength.

You may also deliberately choose as a mentee someone who has skills to boost another department that is important to the success of yours. Sales managers, for example, are very keen to get people they can do business with overseeing the work of the graphics department. Or indeed you may want to put your own person into the graphics department, because you want to move the existing head upwards, without weakening her department by her departure.

Being in the same work environment also means that you have to be doubly sure of the capacity of your mentee, since you will be held responsible for her, her failures as well as her successes. This will also happen with a mentee beyond the boundaries of your own organisation, but the repercussions on your own reputation are likely to be less direct. And if you are grooming your mentee so that she can take your place while you attend to your own future, you have to be triply sure of her.

You must also be absolutely certain of the degree to which she can respect confidentiality, since you will often find yourself giving her information which could be sensitive in terms of the company's future, and your place in it. You will doubtless also often reveal confidential information about yourself when you are just relaxing, or letting her know about your weaknesses in order not to let her make the same mistake. Your judgement is therefore crucial. Your reputation is on the line, inside or outside the organisation.

Mutual Expectation
It will be clear from what we have said above that you need to be sure of what it is that you each want out of your relationship. Your mentee can be very useful to you, whether or not you are both in the same company. If she is, she can help you run your show the way you want it run, and help you to get promotion and more power in the process.

What are you giving her in return? Is she convinced that in serving your purposes she is also serving her own, that she is learning skills and getting experience which will enhance her own future? Some of this mutual expectation and mutual satisfaction can be determined by finger-tip feeling, but in some cases it might be helpful to put down on paper what each of you wants and see if you can come to some mutually acceptable arrangement. This is what is meant by a mentoring contract, and it is particularly useful in a formal mentoring scheme where you come together because the scheme exists, rather than because you have grown together naturally.

Personality Factors

We now turn to those personal characteristics so important in any human relationship. Mentoring is a personal relationship involving real people, beings with emotions as well as work needs. That means that chemistry is involved. Bowen uses the images of infatuation and love to describe various stages of the mentoring relationship. While I wouldn't always go that far, I see what he means. To continue this image briefly, it confirms that we can all mentor if we find the right person to be our mentee, if what we have to offer is wanted by someone who crosses our path looking for just that. But it also suggests that no matter how good the individual quality of the two people concerned, the personal chemistry may not be right between them, and the whole thing will end in an anti-climax, if not utter disaster.

But the imagery of love can only take us so far. Our emotions are only one part of the picture, for in mentoring we are dealing with adult beings whose primary concern is career development, whether they are offering help or seeking help from others, or both, concurrently or consecutively. So while a good chemistry mix is a bonus, it is not the only factor. The cold light of reason has its part to play.

Plenty of people have told me that they don't really like their mentors as people but that they respect them and acknowledge that they have helped them to get on. Others do not like their mentees or do not agree with them politically, but they know that they can be relied on to do a good job, and are exactly what is needed to take over division X and pull it into shape.

Competence in Mentoring

Let us briefly recap what mentors can do for their mentees. We can help them see:

- Where they are.
- What options for the future are open to them.
- Which options they want to pursue.
- What routes they have to travel to get there.
- What milestones they must pass on the way.
- What knowledge, facilities, equipment, experiences they need to get there.

In short, we can help them to establish their needs and set their goals. Then we can help them to achieve those goals.

In order to do this we need to be competent at two levels of mentoring activity. Firstly, we must ourselves know, at least in the abstract, what developmental routes people can follow to achieve success. Secondly, we have to have adequate powers of perception to see where people are at, and where they might be able to go; adequate powers of persuasion to show them where they can get to and how, if they want to; and adequate sensitivity to pull back when we are not wanted or not necessary.

Selecting the Path

At the first level we need a map in our head of developmental pathways, or a checklist of developmental waystages. In some cases mentors are helped in this by companies which have a developmental programme through which all employees wanting to climb that corporate ladder must pass. All that the mentor has to do technically is help her mentee through each of these stages. And if no such programme exists then the mentor must draw up her own checklist and guide her mentee along the route to success.

But it is not as simple as that. Mentoring is not about helping people jump through hoops, though certainly that comes into it. Mentoring is about people and value judgements, and that means that emotional and ethical considerations come into play. What is success for one person is misery to another, and we have to know the difference. We have to judge which of all the pathways that our mentee could in principle follow are appropriate for her, and which we will encourage her to follow, and at what stage in her development.

It is here that we need to draw on the second level of mentoring competence.

Perceptive Mentoring

In order to make the right decisions about the support we give our mentees we must be receptive to all the signs that a mentee is giving out about her capacity, her desires, her problems, etc. which may influence our choices. We must observe, watch and listen; ask pertinent questions, and listen to the answers; provide learning opportunities and assess the results; spot the gaps, and take steps to fill them.

All this implies that we must work on ourselves and our mentoring competences if we are to mentor properly, for concepts of success change, managerial styles change, the whole business culture changes, techniques of counselling develop, and we must not be caught napping. Nor must we allow our sensitivity to be dulled.

Some mentoring schemes, as we shall see later, provide training for mentors, to induct them and keep them up to date. But if we do not have access to this training, or to supplement it, we must continue to network, not only to further our own career but to further our ability to mentor. We must observe other people in action, and talk to them about the actions they take, the decisions they make and the rationale underlying all this. We can also ask for help with a problem, in getting a mentee over a particular hurdle.

The networks which will help you to mentor are diverse. I remember being terribly impressed by a man I observed teaching would-be Samaritans the techniques of eliciting vital information from desperate telephone callers. Whilst mentors are mercifully not often confronted with matters of life or death, they are often faced with mentees who cannot, for reasons of perspective or inhibition, formulate their own problems. As mentors we must be able to do this for them, to be able to provide the help they need.

Pride and Joy

Finally, I would like to deal with what is a cause for concern to some mentors. Some people worry that it is somehow not quite right to feel any satisfaction when their mentee has done well. This sensation is perfectly justifiable. There is nothing immodest or unpleasantly self-congratulatory about it. It is legitimate for fathers and mothers to feel this about the success of their off-spring, and it is legitimate for us as mentors too. We have real reason to feel satisfaction in their achievement. It is OK to say with pride, 'I was her mentor.'

Elizabeth Dole

Elizabeth Dole has climbed very high in her political career: she is Secretary of Labor in the Bush Administration. In 1988 she was named by the Gallup Poll as one of the world's ten most admired women. Very early on she realised the importance of networking and mentoring. During one summer when she was working for a Senator, she made a point of approaching several prominent women in government to get their professional guidance. They were all helpful, but the one who did most for her was Senator Margaret Chase Smith. It was she who suggested that the aspiring politician Elizabeth Dole should bolster her education by getting a law degree, which she did, and which has proved invaluable to her in the jobs she has subsequently had in government service.

Elizabeth Dole now takes very seriously the role of encouraging and mentoring other women who seek a similar career. She was a founder member of 'Executive Women in Government', a club which helps younger women who want to go into government, giving them information and advice on how to avoid certain pitfalls. It also provides network support for women in decision-making positions, enabling them to relate to one another across government. The purpose of this is to help women form the kinds of informal contacts which men have found so vital.

'Such networking,' she says, 'is also a key to the success of women in private enterprise. Decades of male domination of top corporate positions have ensured that the existing informal network system is often for men only. Days at the golf course, weekends at the hunting lodge, and afternoons at the club still close out women.'

She sees this as one of the barriers which prevent women from getting through the glass ceiling to the very top. 'My objective as Secretary of Labor is to look through this glass ceiling, to see who is on the other side, and to serve as a catalyst for change in ensuring women equal access to senior management employment opportunities. We aim to give a "wake-up" call to businesses, telling them that they will miss the boat if they don't realise that the next "fair-haired boy" of their organisation just might be a woman.'

(Quotation taken from a speech made at the Nancy Astor Dinner in 1990, organised by the 300 Group.)

CHAPTER 6

The Benefits of Mentoring

We have seen in earlier chapters the kinds of benefit that networking and being mentored can bring. The value of each benefit is
relative, depending on where people are in their career and what
they want out of life in general. The same applies to the benefits
that a mentor derives from being in a mentoring relationship.
These benefits vary according to the nature of the relationship you
have with your mentee, the mutual trust and interdependence that
exist between you, the length of time you have known each other,
whether you both work in the same organisation, your personal
value system, your personality characteristics, etc. Benefits exist at
all levels.

Psychosocial Benefits

All the benefits are life-enhancing in the sense that they contribute
to our growth as people, what we have previously labelled
psychosocial. But there are few psychosocial benefits that do not
also make us better mentors, therefore better employees and of
greater value to our company and worthy of promotion. The
psychosocial benefits therefore have career implications. But there
are some benefits of having a mentee that are of more direct value
than others in helping us to develop our own careers – these have
been called the career benefits and are discussed later.

Increased Understanding
One of the most important benefits to be derived from mentoring
others is the greater understanding that you gain of your own

behaviour, often intuitive, your own actions and decisions, when you have to explain them to less experienced people. Such learning can help us to be more aware of our actions in future, and maybe even improve on them in the light of our own greater understanding.

This learning occurs at all levels: at policy level (altering the company structure to gain tax advantages, hiving off certain activities to a newly created charity and covenanting profits to it), or at a very low technical level.

I remember coaching someone in the skills of chairing a committee, something she needed to learn for a possible promotion to regional manager in a computer applications consultancy. I managed to observe her in action, and went cold when she used her gavel to maintain order twice in a short meeting. This was a straightforward gut reaction on my part: I knew beyond any denying that what she was doing was wrong, and quite counterproductive, and told her so. She was totally perplexed at my criticism, feeling that by the use of the gavel she had been showing assertively that she was boss. I then had the job of analysing all the clues that had caused my intuitive reaction, in order to explain the evidence to her.

To me the use of the gavel indicated that she had lost control, and the pulling of rank (the unabashed reliance on the external symbol of authority) to regain it displayed a weakness rather than a strength. The shocked reaction of other people, the look on their faces and their drawing back in their chairs, showed me that her behaviour had been judged officious rather than authoritative, and they resented both the noise and the behaviour. They had been unruly, but not rebellious, and the problem would have disappeared on both occasions if she had just waited patiently and silently for the storm to blow itself out.

She further protested to me that she had needed to use the gavel to attract the attention of the people spread widely about the room, seated at several little tables covered with green baize. But she could have forestalled the problem by having the tables brought together before the meeting began, thus reducing the space over which she had visibly and audibly to exercise control.

Behaviour Modification

Another occasion concerned with pulling rank gave me the opportunity to examine and modify my *own* behaviour. Many years ago someone I was mentoring asked me to approve a report she had just written, just as I was leaving for an important meeting. It was a mess, so I gave her a few brief hints on what was wrong and gave her a similar report so that she could copy the company format. She looked at it and asked, 'Why do you want it done this way?' I said 'Because I want it done that way' and then I left. My behaviour had been rude and my explanation inadequate, quite unsuitable in one meant to be training another. Later I apologised and we were able to repair the damage I had caused to her sense of self-worth and to our relationship. She had been asking for more help than I had had time to give her at that particular stage, and I was irritated that she wasn't sensitive to my needs at that moment as sensitivity was one of the things I was trying to teach her. At the very least I should have said 'I haven't got time to explain now. For the moment, will you just do it this way, and we'll talk about it later.'

However, I should have made sure that she knew that I was busy that morning and not available for discussion and I shouldn't have expected her to read my mind. It was an important lesson for me and one often experienced by new mentors.

Understanding Learning Needs

Teaching a mentee forces you to look at things from all sorts of different angles. It is particularly beneficial to have a mentee who asks you what she wants to know, for this allows you to gain an insight into the way her mind is working, and what guidance she needs.

Consider the following question: 'You know the other day when Tom claimed that he had initiated the Brussels idea. Why did you let him get away with it? Why didn't you say it had been your idea all along?'

From this you hear her moral outrage that ideas were wrongly credited. But you also hear that she is still weak in understanding negotiation and power play. For you this is by now second nature, so you may have overlooked her learning needs in those areas. The needs of our mentees are a constant spur to our own continued learning and developing, not always in areas which we could have predicted.

Turning Mistakes to Profit

As mentors we get satisfaction in stopping people from making the mistakes we have made, or at least in alerting them to the kinds of things that can go wrong if they are not very careful. We have all made wrong moves, said the wrong thing, failed to do something, and it brings a kind of cosmic legitimacy to those experiences if they can be shown not to have been in vain, if they can be turned to profit in someone else's life. The following quotation says it all:

'My personal hell was worthwhile because she has profited from my errors.' This is from a woman who had been a senior personnel officer in several large companies before taking up a position as a university lecturer. Despite her thoroughly grounded knowledge of her subject and her highly acclaimed ability as a teacher, and despite several frustrated applications, she was never promoted to a senior position. Her error had been in failing to recognise, until it was too late, that university values for promotion are different from those in industry. She had concentrated on developing her students, and neglected to establish a power base among academic colleagues. She had published little, and therefore, in the power terms of a university, had little clout. The situation was a disgrace, but the younger women in her department, staff and students, learned from this, and benefitted from her tragedy.

This point was specifically addressed by Reich in his survey of 520 executives. He discovered that senior people had realised the importance of political *nous* throughout their careers and passed this knowledge on to their mentees, even when they themselves had not received this benefit from their own mentors: 84 per cent of his respondents advised their mentees in this area, while only 64 per cent had received such guidance themselves (Reich, p43).

Self-Worth

Being sought out by younger people gives you a sense of your own self-worth. If people on their way up come to you for help of whatever kind, then that reinforces the values of your experience and gives you a sense of doing the right thing, having a place in the order of things. We all of us have a creative need to pass something on to the next generation, and seeing our experience have

135

meaning for our mentees satisfies that urge. This is a particularly important benefit of mentoring for senior people who are at a career standstill, 'plateaued' managers to use the American jargon. There are many reasons for not being able to make progress. There may, for example, be no room above them in their own company, so they can only progress by moving elsewhere.

But there are often reasons for not moving elsewhere, so the people concerned are stuck, and the sensation of no longer being able to make progress is very depressing. Having a mentee in such circumstances can be really life enhancing. Although your progress up one ladder has come to an end, you can progress up another, furthering a new career in developing other people, passing on your valuable experience and helping them progress. This is also very important as a second career for retired people, with a wealth of experience, and no one to pass it on to. Such women are invaluable as consultants or advisers, or even just as active members of women's professional organisations where there are younger women just waiting to lap up their knowledge and skills.

As in so many other things, Eleanor Macdonald is a role-model also in this. At the age of 59 she was neither plateaued nor retired, but when the circumstances of her company were changed by world events, she took the opportunity to take stock of what she wanted for the rest of her life. She decided to opt for early retirement and then embarked on a second career running a training consultancy, passing on the wealth of her experience to women from many different job areas throughout the world. It was about this time that she also founded Women in Management so that women could meet and share common problems and derive mutual benefits. Eleanor has been mentoring women ever since.

Securing the Future

Another benefit of mentoring is a sort of philosophic peace of mind, a security that comes of knowing that your work will continue because you have developed people who value it and will propagate it, probably developing your ideas beyond what you found possible at the time.

This happens with a line of work, a way of behaving, a set of values. It is very obvious in the case of people like Florence Nightingale, whose vision, determination and training of others led to the profession of nursing as we know it today. In more recent times, but also ironically helped by the demands of war, women in the armed services opened up new ways for women to serve their country, battling to eliminate discrimination where there was no justification for it. They have brought on women (and men) who share their vision, to the point where we now have women helicopter pilots who may be deployed in combat zones, and where women in the navy may serve aboard ship rather than remain land-based.

Other women have secured the future of their ideas in ways much less spectacular, but just as revolutionary, by passing on their personal value system to their mentees, showing them for example that it is far more decent and productive to treat fellow workers as sensitive and creative human beings rather than disposable insensient operatives.

Pride in the Product

It is good to be able to watch someone's progress, and see her achieve great things. As mentors we get a legitimate satisfaction out of our teaching, out of providing an environment in which our mentees can learn and grow, and then seeing their efforts rewarded time and again, even climbing beyond us in a certain sense. And it is OK to have a parent-like feeling of pride, knowing that there is something of us in them that is being silently acknowledged in the rewards they receive.

Direct Career Benefits

It is common for mentors to claim that they have gained insights into their own career future by talking to their mentees and helping them to map out the options for their future, and the steps they can take to get there. As you help them to consider their present and past satisfactions, and future needs and desires, you reflect on your own situation and introduce into your own options a clarity found only in explaining things to others. You also understand what benefits you gain from being a mentor to others.

Feedback

Thinking through an action or a policy in sufficient detail to instruct your mentee in smart ways of behaving gives you the opportunity to adapt or alter your decision before implementing it. For example, you may be explaining the factors which have led you to choose a given date for a major conference when you suddenly realise that you haven't properly taken into account the lead time of the publications in which you will be advertising it. This is self-feedback.

But you can also learn from the comments of your mentees. At a very simple level I have had mentees who have suggested to me that the results of a survey could be better presented by using a particular kind of graph. I have also had major help from them when they have suggested for example that by asking an additional question in a survey form I would be able to make the core information I was seeking more important in marketing terms. This kind of exchange is exceedingly useful, resulting from the close interaction of someone well-experienced, competent and confident, with someone less of all these things, but bright and fresh and able to bring a new perspective to bear.

Testing Ideas

Some mentors use their mentees to minimise the risk of introducing something new. A mentor may have a very new idea she wishes to use for the recruitment literature but may be uncertain about the client's reaction. She can send her mentee off with it to test the waters. If the client reacts favourably, then the project goes ahead and the team takes the credit. If not, no harm is done to the reputation of the mentor since it will be assumed that the mentee was the one who still needs a bit more training.

This use of more junior staff happens all the time in business, whether in commercial or non-profit-making organisations. Whether or not it is a proper way to behave depends on the relationship between the two people, what they want from each other and the price they are prepared to pay. It has advantages for both if handled decently. For the mentee it can be vital training. For the mentor, it stops her from making a public mistake, with a client, partner or senior.

It is not always necessary to send your ideas out with your mentees to test the waters. You can also do it just by having a chat, and seeing how your mentee – younger, fresher, closer to the ground – reacts. This can happen with ideas for new products, plans for restructuring, new bonus schemes, new training schemes, etc. Again it minimises the risk and helps to prevent you from taking a wrong turn before you are very far down the road.

Liberation Through Delegation

In the instances above we see vital but indirect support being provided from below in order to help a mentor get a job done. But it is also common for the mentor and mentee to work together on the same project, for them to share the load. When a mentor is, say, designing new recruitment literature for a client, it is extremely useful if she has a mentee on whom she can rely to do some of the actual work for her, from taking the brief from the client to doing paste-ups or presenting drafts for feedback. This is all part of the training process for the mentee, but it frees the mentor to go out and look for other clients, or develop other parts of her work, thus her career.

Increased Power Base

Our power base depends not only on who we know in the ranks above us, but who and how many people support us from below. In political language, whose vote we can count on.

One of the consequences of helping others is that we increase the number of people who have reason to believe in our ability. They will therefore support us, not in the nasty sense that they 'owe us something', but because they know we deliver the goods. And the more we network and achieve high visibility helping and supporting others, the more we put round the story that we are the right person for the next job. This is a major area of career development that women forget to attend to, so if they can be convinced that this sort of advantage quite legitimately flows from helping others so much the better for them and their potential mentees.

The grapevine is very important in letting very senior people know from the bottom up who is worth putting into top positions. Organisations often deliberately set out (discreetly of course) to canvas opinion about how junior staff feel towards their seniors. And only this week I have been told by a friend that an outplacement agency with whom she has registered (as a result of a foreign buy-out) wanted to interview people who have worked *for* her in the past, rather than the other way round! She is known to have been a generous mentor to many younger people, women and men, and certainly the reports that they give of her as a boss and employer will be favourable.

Increased Performance

Another way in which the power base of mentors grows is that people who want to get to the top, and who want the right kind of help in getting to the top, ask to work with them. I have seen this happen time and again, even with people who are reckoned to be fairly uncompromising in human terms, but who can teach people the ropes. People clamour to be put with mentors who have a reputation for helping others get results. This means that bright and ambitious people, people who want to learn, offer their services to you. And there is no doubt that if you are working closely with someone who is good, then the sum product from two individuals is closer to three than it is to two. They provide you with reliable support, new ideas, perspectives and information. Working with high performers is extremely stimulating and challenging, helping you to be on top form and helping your department to produce good work. All of which is important for your own promotion.

Expansion of networks

In our own careers we have learned the importance of networks, and mentoring others can take us into other networks to which we would not have access but for them. For example, our mentees ask us to go and talk to their networks about our work and experience, or they invite us to events, conferences, receptions. Sometimes they want to thank us for our interest in them; sometimes they want us to hold their hand; sometimes they want to boost their own importance in the eyes of the people who will be there. Sometimes it is conscious. It doesn't matter. The benefits are mutual.

Access to Resources

In order to get a job done properly, or better than a competing individual or agency, it is vital to have access to appropriate resources: facilities, equipment, information and funding. In earlier chapters we noted that mentors often help mentees by making sure that they have access to the resources they need. But it also happens that mentees work in organisations where they have better resources, or easier access to them, than their mentor. In my own case, for example, I have been able to make use of specialist library *facilities* to which my mentees have easier access than me. They put themselves out for me, as I do with people who have been helpful to me.

Access to appropriate *equipment* is also vital. Mentors needing to have data analysed on fast and powerful computers can often rely on mentees to get work done for them. Or they can make use of very sophisticated graphics programmes not available in their own company. Or they can get their hands on the latest video equipment for new training projects, or transport to meet a particular need.

Accurate *information* can also be supplied by mentees. Say that the graphics department has got some new equipment they are very proud of. You need to know how long it will be before it is up and running, for you want some presentation work done, and you don't know whether to send it outside, or wait to have it done in-house. The head of graphics is not saying anything helpful about delays, but if you happen to have a (former) mentee in that department the problem disappears, and you can make your decision in the light of accurate information.

And *funding* can be obtained from mentees. The most obvious example of this is former students (mentees) being encouraged by tutors (mentors) to cough up money to support a new project, a course or even a college at their old school or university where their mentors taught. But campaigns, enquiries, training schemes have been funded by mentees who use their own money, or funds over which they have control, to help a mentor in her new venture.

All this is very important for mentors in employment, to help them do a job better or faster, to help them up their own promotion ladder. Mentors typically start mentoring in their mid- to late-thirties, and can build up a large network of mentees over the years. They develop a great pyramid of people below them pushing them up. But this kind of support is absolutely vital for those in self-employment who do not have the resources available to big corporations. Independent consultants have often had work put their way by mentees who are not just grateful for earlier help, but who know with certainty that their consultant will deliver.

Reputation as Starmaker

Good mentors get a reputation as a starmaker. When your mentee introduces you as 'the person to whom I owe everything', it may not be true but it does give you a warm glow. More practically, starmakers are awarded all sorts of privileges, given information and access to facilities, invited to join clubs, etc. because starmakers are seen as people of vision and power, and should be nourished, for who knows when they might be needed.

In many organisations it is good to be known as a starmaker, and can guarantee your own position. It is vital for any company to know that it has on its staff people 'who can pick a good one', people good at spotting talent and who will train junior people in the skills and culture needed in that particular company. Word gets round about such people because they are so valuable. In general terms they may continue to rise within the company, but even if in purely job terms they are not expected to climb higher they are often retained with a new job title, when others are at a standstill or asked to look elsewhere. Indeed, someone with a reputation as a starmaker may find it easier to get work with another organisation, for they too want good talent spotters, people who can bring on the next generation.

Grooming a Successor

Some people get trapped in a particular position, not because they are not good enough to be promoted, but because they do their own current job too well. There is no one that good to replace them. This makes it difficult for them to get leave for a sabbatical year, for example, or an extended work trip away, or even for a competitive yacht-trip round the world. Smart mentors therefore develop their mentee to do that same job well, so that the mentor can be promoted out, and the mentee promoted in. The company will know that the job is in good hands, because she will have told them.

Empire Building

Zey sees all career benefits as feeders of one major benefit:

> By far the greatest benefit that mentoring can bring to a senior manager's success is in the area of empire building. The road to

142

success lies open to the mentor who realises that the strong type of influence network is composed of protégés whom he can place permanently throughout the organisation (p82, *The Mentor Connection*).

Zey's research concentrated on mentoring in large companies with mentor and mentee working in partnership in the same company, the companies concerned 'growing their own', promoting from amongst their own ranks, rather than buying in from outside. Indeed, a good deal of the American literature on mentoring at work relies on workplace studies with mentor and mentee in the same establishment.

Some of the mentors on whose experience I have drawn work in such companies, but much of the mentoring I have learned about takes place beyond company boundaries, from company to company, in formally established networking organisations, between counsellor and client or purely informally. This makes a direct correlation between mentoring and promotion for either party difficult to establish. But my mentors nevertheless claim career benefits from having mentored junior people, although they do not use the same blunt expression of 'empire building' as Zey.

We must at least consider whether we are here dealing with differences of gender and culture. I set out deliberately to examine the experiences of women at work in the British context, whereas Zey and most others I have consulted review mixed groups in North America. It is theoretically possible that the British as distinct from Americans, and women as distinct from mixed gender groups, would not offer the concept of 'empire building' as a legitimate advantage of mentoring. It may seem, for British women, a little too aggressive. In our more reticent culture we are more likely to want to do a thing because it is intrinsically good, and then be glad if the consequences also benefit us, rather than the other way round. But the career benefits for mentors exist nevertheless, for women, for men, in Britain and America, within companies, and across company boundaries, however delicately we refer to them.

Linda Kelsey

The world of journalism is usually reckoned to be a pretty cut-throat place with lots of queen bees of both sexes intent only on their own progress and not caring who they step on to get their story out first. But a number of women journalists I have spoken to paint an entirely different picture. They have had good help and guidance from senior women colleagues, and in several instances have had long-term mentoring relationships with other women.

Linda Kelsey in a case in point. She had the good fortune to be mentored by Maggie Goodman, now the editor of *Hello*. They met when Linda joined *Cosmopolitan* magazine, where Maggie was already deputy editor. Despite the traditional image of ambitious journalists, Linda was actually quite shy and unsure of herself. She benefitted enormously from Maggie's expressed confidence in her. Maggie gave her the most precious of commodities, time, guided her in the technical details of her job, and helped her handle aspects that terrified her. Maggie was also an important role model for Linda, being successful herself, and having a quiet authority which Linda admired and respected.

Maggie later left *Cosmopolitan* and set up *Company*. But Linda went with her, becoming deputy editor. Later still Linda went back to *Cosmo* to become editor. And Maggie was very pleased for her, glad that the potential which she had noticed much earlier was being acknowledged and rewarded by other people. She felt justified in her judgement. Now that Maggie has moved on to *Hello*, and Linda has become editor of *She*, their professional relationship has changed to one of equality. But Linda is happy to recall the help she got from Maggie on the way, and Maggie insists that she too was helped in her career by having Linda with her. They are both hard-working women who serve as good role models for others to follow. Both are generous in the help they give.

(With grateful acknowledgement to Elaine Gallagher, *qv*.)

CHAPTER 7

Mentoring Schemes

There are a number of formal training or development schemes in which mentoring plays a role. In some cases these involve career development programmes where mentoring is provided as a support in getting through the programme. But other schemes see mentoring as a primary tool, and are designed specifically to encourage its use. We shall look at both types of scheme in this chapter. Except where specified, the schemes are available to men and women alike.

Formal schemes can be run by employers or others. They can be run in-house, on the company's premises, or out-house in training establishments. They are to be found in commercial corporations at international and national level, in areas which include administration, banking, information technology, health care, the law, management consulting, production, marketing, recruitment, retailing, etc. They can also be found in non-profit-making areas like educational institutions and within education authorities. But formal mentoring is also found outside company structures, in ex-corporate arrangements, like professional associations, women's networks, private counselling programmes, and competitions.

Development Programmes

In-house mentoring schemes often form part of a personal development programme expected to last a number of years. A typical programme lists the knowledge and experience that an employee is expected to develop if she is to make progress in the company. These development programmes include courses and

145

possibly examinations, work experience and work shadowing in given departments, visits to other companies or other countries etc. The programmes can often be taken at the employees' own pace, and typically take between three and six years. Some people will romp through, whilst others will never complete them.

These development programmes usually make provision for personal development advisers. These advisers are usually senior operational members of the company. Although the term mentor is rarely used, advisers are expected to perform many of the functions that we have seen mentors performing. They are meant to oversee and encourage the people assigned to them. They help them decide how many of the units of the programme they should tackle at any one time, what visits to go on, the order in which they should apply to various departments, etc.

Advisers are generally expected to offer advice on the kind of dress and behaviour that is required in that particular company, in other words to help the individual understand and adapt to company culture. They are also meant to help their charges analyse their own needs and encourage them to discuss their weaknesses and seek remedies. And they should also help them with their long-term career goals with the company. Many personal advisers also help with 'life problems', domestic difficulties, ethical concerns, etc.

Although in many cases the programmes can theoretically be entered by any employee at whatever grade, in practice they are usually followed by people who have come into the company after completing a degree course, as so-called 'graduate entrants'. But it can and does happen that others are encouraged to take part. Line managers (or appraisors, where appraisal schemes exist) are often asked to recommend likely candidates to enter, even if their work experience to date wouldn't normally indicate suitability. I am delighted to say that I know of one bank where a suitable candidate has been found lurking among the forty-year-old women returners in a clerical position.

Some development programmes are designed to get good people, people of potentially outstanding value to the company, into responsible positions fast. They are therefore called 'the fast track'. Often these are available only to those who have been assessed at the beginning of their career with the company as 'high achievers'. Some companies have a 'very fast track', what I have heard called a 'luxury service for the minority'. One particular company assigns people to this very fast track right at the beginning of their career, before they have proved their value as employees. Cross-over to this very fast track is virtually impossible for existing employees. The personal advisers (mentors) in this scheme are still operational members of the company, but they are extremely senior people. They take their charges with them into their own departments to give them work-shadowing experience, and make sure that they get very good supervision and encouragement in all the other departments in which they work to gain experience. This is a very high pressure scheme, and the personal adviser acts as mentor, appraisor and assessor.

To my mind there is a serious weakness here, for the employee in this scheme does not have a chance to admit a weakness, other than to diagnose a shortcoming in say commercial law and to request further experience in that area. She cannot say entirely confidentially, as she could to a mentor who is primarily helping rather than judging her, that she is really in despair about commercial law and doesn't think she is going to pass. There is also a danger that she will bottle up personal problems in case a temporary difficulty could lead to a judgement of instability or long-term failure. If a personal adviser cannot be used as a confidential adviser without repercussions, then she is not able to perform a vital function of mentoring.

This problem could be overcome if the company were to implement the company counsellor schemes now being introduced into Britain. Some companies recognise that unhappiness in their employees, no matter how caused, affects their productive capacity, so they provide private and confidential counselling with a psychologist or psychotherapist, not just the company doctor or nurse whose responsibilities lie elsewhere. Such a counsellor can take over one aspect of mentoring, but given the number of people whom they have to see, it is unlikely that they will have time to be fully-fledged mentors (see Sidney and Phillips, and Jarvie and Matthews).

In another company, strongly influenced by its American parent, the personal adviser scheme is very highly developed, and continues even after a formal training programme has long been completed. Right up to grades immediately below chief executive level employees have personal advisers and they are expected to use them. One of the purposes of this is to relieve stress, to give a person with a lot of responsibility a chance to discuss things, and to seek psychological support when it is needed. This is different from chatting things over with the boss when you are faced by a number of options. It is not intended to take operational responsibility away from senior people, but to give them the chance to sit back and take stock – about anything, work, home, children, future, etc. This can only work where there is a very high level of acceptance of the company culture, and an equally high level of trust from one senior person to another. But the rewards for company loyalty are great indeed in this organisation, and the people who don't fit in are weeded out at an early stage.

Schemes without a Development Programme

In-house mentoring does not have to be tied to a grand scale development programme. It can stand alone as the primary development technique. Employees are selected for particular development on the basis of annual assessments and other forms of observation. They are assigned a mentor for a given period, say for two years, who is expected to perform the usual mentoring functions. The relationship may continue after that time, but it only does so because both partners want it. Sometimes mentees are able to choose a mentor from any of the senior people they know, or they choose from a panel. Together with their mentor they work through the same sort of thing as we have seen set out above, but the programme would be designed with the individual in mind.

Before leaving this topic I feel impelled to mention a situation reported by Reich: 'One company assigned senior executives to high-potential employees who may or may not know that the executives are their mentors' (p45, 'Executive Views from Both Sides of Mentoring'). If there is a point to this, I don't know what it is.

Induction Schemes

Induction schemes are usually run in-house, but are usually of shorter duration than others indicated above. They are designed to introduce new entrants to a profession or grade and sometimes include mentors. I have found examples in several areas of education.

Further and Higher Education

Traditionally university lecturers have clung tenaciously to their rights of autonomy as researchers and teachers, and fiercely fought off any attempt to 'train' them. Whilst a training programme is still not universal, it has nevertheless been accepted in many institutions that some form of guidance is appropriate, particularly since a professional qualification in teaching is not necessary for teachers in higher education. A senior person, often called a supervisor, is appointed by the relevant committee on the recommendation of the Head of Department, to aid the development of someone new to the profession, to help her establish priorities in her teaching and research, and to help her improve her actual teaching techniques. This supervisor is also expected to give such guidance as may be necessary to ensure that the junior lecturer publishes enough and in the right journals, to be considered worthy of permanent appointment. She should also be helped to get to conferences and give papers at the 'right' conferences, to raise her visibility in other words, so as to be seen to be worthy of advancement. This is especially important for academics where advancement is frequently by movement from one institution to another, particularly at the higher levels.

This scheme can be advantageous to both parties. They can publish papers together, the older one actually being asked by an editor to produce something, thus guaranteed publication, and the younger one getting the chance to have her name associated with someone well recognised in the field. The older person can sponsor the younger one at conferences, or at promotion committees, or give suitable references for external promotion. Supervisor and junior can become good friends, and give each other professional and personal support.

Such a scheme can also be disastrous. In some cases the people assigned to supervise younger staff are selected on the basis of their subject knowledge rather than their suitability to induct younger colleagues. Having had no training themselves, they may feel little sympathy with training. Or they may resent having this extra burden thrust upon them, when what they really want to be doing is research and publish their own work. It can also happen that the older one abuses the younger one, regarding her as an assistant, and paying little attention to her personal needs. I have also seen it happen in the gentle groves of academe that bad references have been given to keep a promising younger colleague in the department, rather than let her go elsewhere.

Local Education Authority

Certain education authorities have mentors in their induction schemes for head teachers and education officers.

Head Teachers Head teachers in a school can be very isolated. Whilst the staff can be very supportive, they do not have the same type of managerial responsibility. And this is considerable, especially since the introduction of LMS, local management of schools, under which heads and their governing body also have financial and recruitment obligations previously borne by the Education Authority. Some Education Authorities have tried to provide help for their new heads by specifying established heads to whom they can turn as mentors.

In a particular authority an established and respected head teacher is nominated to take an active part in the first selection interview, but plays no part thereafter until someone is appointed. This person then becomes the mentor for the person appointed, and is then expected to make contact, either on the phone or by letter, saying that she is available for consultation if required. And the new head may then follow this up or not. She can visit the mentor's school and learn how the mentor has tackled certain problems. She can chat about problems in general, or seek specific advice, putting say certain development plans to her for comment. The purpose of having a mentor is to help the new head find her feet, adjust to the new role, avoid some of the pitfalls, get moral or practical support, and all totally confidentially. The mentor head is not there to judge or report to the Authority but to offer help.

There doesn't need to be love for this relationship to work, but there does need to be a degree of both common sense and respect. I was told of one situation where the appropriate education officer told an incoming deputy head that she 'could have Mrs X as a mentor if she liked'. But Mrs X made no contact of any kind, and the deputy head was left floundering, not feeling it appropriate to initiate contact herself. She is now trying to get out of teaching.

Education Officers   Another Education Authority has introduced a mentoring scheme to help with the induction of Education Officers. Senior Education Officers are designated mentors, and are expected to induct new EOS, helping them work through a set programme of experience and knowledge. Under this scheme training is also given to the mentors to help them do their job properly, and a very detailed programme is set out, including workshops, discussion groups, written support materials for mentors, trainers, etc (see LGTB).

Her Majesty's Inspectorate

Being an HMI can be tricky. HMIS have a responsible and somewhat ambivalent task, having in a sense to ensure that educational provision conforms to the relevant legislation, but also providing government with independent advice on changes in practice or policy. They visit educational establishments all over the country, assess them and comment, if necessary making recommendations for change. They have some administrative support from a regional centre, but basically work from home, in isolation from peers with whom they can discuss their work. New entrants have an induction course right at the beginning, but to provide ongoing support an established HMI is assigned as a mentor, to help her organise her workload for at least the first few months, to provide supervision, to accompany her on visits and give any other kind of support that is necessary. But this mentor also has a reporting function, and is expected to comment on the suitability of the HMI (Lawton and Gordon, p120).

Guardian Angel

A mentoring scheme very different in structure from what we have seen above is the guardian angel scheme run by the Institute of Translation and Interpreting. It is administered by a professional association rather than an employer, but is close to an apprenticeship in concept. The ITI is a professional association representing both staff and freelance translators and interpreters. The guardian angel scheme was started informally, but was later established as a service to members to which all had access if they wished. One

151

purpose of the scheme is to combat the isolation felt by translators working freelance, often from home or libraries, where contact with other professionals is limited. They may never even see the people who use their services, much of their work being sent through the post or faxed to their clients or the agencies they work for.

A fledgling translator is paired with a guardian angel, a well established translator. As far as possible people with the same language speciality are put together. The fledgling may be a fairly recent graduate, or someone new to the translation profession after some years in another, for example in the civil service. Fledglings learn from their guardian angels not only technical points of translation and how to get up speed, what sources of information are best, how to establish glossaries, etc; but also how to run their business, from acquiring equipment, to getting clients and keeping accounts. Some GAS actually pass on work to their fledglings when they can't handle all of it.

In return for this fledglings perform a range of services for guardian angels, from running errands like photocopying and ordering a courier bike, to checking specialist terms, to doing a first draft of a translation for a GA who is in a hurry to get the next text out. This system also allows the fledgling to discuss her concerns about work, or about her career, or her domestic or other worries with someone who has been through similar difficulties. It also allows both fledgling and guardian to have a professional referee, as it were, a partner on whom to try out alternative renderings, and a friend from whom psychological support can be expected when the going gets tough. Several pairs continue to work together over the years after their official pairing has come to an end.

Training

Mentoring is found not only in employment, as above, but in pre-employment training.

Teaching
Teachers being trained to teach in further and adult education establishments will have a mentor as well as a subject tutor,

depending on what Education Authority they train with (see NASD).

Law
It can also be argued that the pupillage system that barristers have to go through can be a mentoring scheme. Primarily this scheme, whereby a 'barrister-in-training' acts as unpaid assistant to a fully-fledged barrister, following her from case to case, is to enable the trainee barrister to learn the conduct of litigation, advocacy, court-room behaviour, etc. But this can develop into mentoring if the guidance goes beyond straight instruction and extends to career advice, life-planning, introduction to networks, etc.

Nursing
The nursing profession has also now introduced the concept of mentoring for student nurses, allowing them to choose a person to 'assist, befriend, guide and counsel', but leaving clinical training to tutors (ENB, p3). There is no standard pattern of behaviour, with each Health Authority making its own arrangements. There is also provision for mentors to be available to nurses throughout their career, after their initial training, with more senior grades taking the mentor role. This is a controversial matter and one issue of *Nursing Times* was devoted to articles on the subject (November 16–22, 1988; see also Morle).

Education

In America quite a lot has been written about the role of mentors in education, one of the most enlightening and inspiring books being by Daloz who recounts his experiences with adult learners. But mentoring is also found in educational schemes in Britain. Tutors have existed in universities from the earliest years, many of them playing a mentoring role. They also exist in, for example, training colleges. In one teacher-training college personal tutors are semi-officially called 'godmothers'!

There are also courses in higher education where certain students are 'sponsored' by employing organisations, and they usually also have a mentor (an extra tutor) appointed by the sponsoring organisation.

153

Sponsorship from business and industry plays a large part in many training schemes that involve mentors. Whilst the sponsoring organisation may retain some training role, providing for example work experience, its main function is to sponsor a student on a place at a named training or research institution. This means that it pays for the training, accommodation, etc that the student receives, usually in return for specific services or favourable publicity.

The Fellowship scheme below is typical of many, and I have chosen it for description here because it also demonstrates the compensatory function that I think important.

The Windsor Fellowship

This is a scheme designed to counteract the waste of talent common in the black community. It was established in 1986 specifically to help contact between employers and young black people with management potential. It is 'interventionist' in that it provides training additional to that received by ordinary students. In this case Fellowships are awarded to students who have already secured a place on a degree course. They receive no financial benefit, but they do get extra tuition and extra guidance at no cost to themselves. They also get a guarantee of paid work placements during the summer vacation with their sponsoring organisation. In addition to giving them some income, this provides valuable employment training and experience of the work environment.

In return these Fellows must undertake two to three hours unpaid community work a week, if possible in the black community where they will 'advertise' their Fellowship and their sponsoring company, in order to raise the profile of the company with potential future employees. They must also attend extra courses designed to encourage their personal development and management skills, like public speaking and decision-making. There is also a compulsory six-day outdoor pursuit course.

The Fellows also get extra mentoring. Like other students they have a tutor who will give advice, support and other kinds of guidance on academic and personal development. But the tutor from their sponsoring organisation, specifically called a mentor, oversees their work and generally performs a mentoring role during their work placements, also remaining in contact to give help and encouragement throughout the academic year.

In such sponsorship schemes the students get many advantages of mentoring, including an introduction to a whole range of new network to which they would not otherwise have access. This results not only from the work experience they have in their own sponsorship companies, but the contacts they make through other Fellows on the scheme when they take part in the additional courses. Bearing in mind that the sponsors of the Windsor Fellowship include Citicorp, the Bank of England, BP, the Transport and General Workers Union and the Home Office, you understand that this can provide an invaluable start to their career.

The Mentor Project

This project is for students below university level. It embodies in principle all the things I have been saying about underachievement and the importance of mentoring in providing compensatory support. Although this particular scheme was set up to cater for the developmental needs of students from the black community in an inner-city area, it demonstrates the same beliefs that I have been expressing about women and proposes some of the same solutions. It aims to help students who show academic promise but who are in danger of underachieving.

The causes of underachievement, whether among women or members of the black community, are many and complex, but two causes in particular are pinpointed by the Mentor Project – the absence of positive personal guidance and the absence of role models. So a personal mentor is provided for each individual student to fill those gaps. All the mentors are black, like the students, and have achieved success in a variety of careers, from law to business. Some of the mentors are very prestigious, like Herman Ouseley, a former Chief Executive of the Inner London Education Authority, and TV reporter and newsreader Jackie Harper. As mentors they undertake a guidance role for each of the students, expanding their horizons, helping them plan their life and career, giving them opportunities for work experience and work shadowing, introducing them to their own personal and professional networks, etc.

One of the primary benefits to students on this project is to see people with whom they can identify, blacks like themselves, achieving success in career terms. They see them in a work environment, cooperating with colleagues, respecting and being

155

respected, taking a leading role, making important decisions, etc. Such role modelling allows the students to develop positive images of black people in our society, rather than just the negative ones often presented.

In addition to this, students on this project are given supplementary educational support. They are already following a course of post-sixteen study, but they are provided with extra activities beyond normal hours – workshops, visits, residential weekends, etc. These cover topics like racial awareness and communication skills, and are intended to reinforce the informal help coming from their mentors, formally encouraging knowledge and skills which should help them achieve employment success within the wider community.

The students on this project have been officially proposed by their 'normal' teachers or lecturers, but the mentors have been found unofficially, usually by word of mouth. Their contribution is enthusiastic and voluntary, but they are not, in the main, educators by training, so they in their turn are given some support to help them meet the responsibility they have undertaken. Together with the directors they discuss the underlying philosophy of the scheme, the part they can play as mentors, and ways in which they might approach their task.

The mentors receive a booklet of suggestions for appropriate activities, discussion topics, and a timetable to give an overall perspective. They are advised to establish early on with their student the ground rules of their partnership, what mentor and mentee can each reasonably expect from the other, how they will proceed, when and where they will meet, etc.

The mentoring pairs are matched according to their social and ethnic background and career area. But it has happened that mentor and mentee hit it off together at an initial social gathering and remain together despite different career areas. And while there are plenty of women mentors on this project, as well as women students, there appears to be no attempt at matching them on a gender basis. The scheme is however sensitive to the particular needs of Bengali women.

Although the details of the actual mentoring are left for the pairs to arrange in the way which best suits them, the project itself is highly structured. It is overseen by a steering committee, and administered by two co-directors. Originally there was also a coordinator to help set it up. It started at North London College in 1989 with support from the Further Education Unit of the Department of Education and Science. It is now funded by Islington Council and LENTA (the London Enterprise Agency) who provide sponsorship from business and industry.

The Mentor Project has been highly praised in the educational press (see Alison Whyte's article in *The Times Educational Supplement*) and elsewhere. Lively first-hand reports from mentors and mentees alike have been brought together in *Mentor Magazine*. This is prefaced by enthusiastic support from Brian Sullivan, who himself benefitted from the guidance of a mentor whom he met during his professional rugby days. He also specifically acknowledges the 'tremendous encouragement' given him by his wife Carole.

This project is delightfully symbolised by its logo: a letter M for Mentoring, formed by a large black person holding hands with a little black person, standing in front of an arrow pointing up. I wish I'd though of that.

Particularly for Women

All the schemes above are for men and women, but there are some run specifically for women, by various organisations.

Women's Networks

Since a major purpose of women's networks is to allow women to come together for a common purpose, informal mentoring often develops between members of such a group. This has been called networking-mentoring by Swoboda and Millar (*qv*). But some women's groups are now deliberately setting up mentoring schemes to bring together women who can offer help and those who are seeking it. One such scheme has recently been set up by the London Branch of Women and Training where they are getting together a panel of women mentors who will be available to mentor younger women in their own field. The London Chamber of Commerce and Industry are actively considering how they could arrange mentoring for their women members. The 300 Group, whose specific aim is to get women into Parliament, are looking at how they can use mentoring to help would-be women MPs. And

157

an investigation into the success level of women entrepreneurs recommended that Business in the Community (BIC) and SCOTBIC should encourage Enterprise Agencies to pilot a scheme whereby existing women entrepreneurs would mentor, and act as role models for others, using a work shadowing scheme (see Carter and Cannon).

The Clairol Scheme

The Clairol company has for many years sponsored training initiatives for women. Amongst them they have a mentoring scheme, where you 'win' your mentor in a competition! You apply by writing about yourself and your plans, and describe how having a mentor could help you meet your development goals. If you are successful in your bid, you are linked up with a mentor and provided with funds to help you travel to meet her for mentoring sessions. So far this scheme is available only in the United States, but I am discussing setting up such a scheme with a national woman's magazine in this country.

It should be noted that in the schemes mentioned above the women who are paired up will not necessarily be from the same job area. Whenever possible an estate agent is paired with an estate agent, but it may be necessary occasionally to choose someone from an allied rather than identical field as a mentor. This is not necessarily a problem. Mentors do not need to know the exact same area as their mentees, for mentoring has many aspects beyond those which rely on subject knowledge.

Re-Training for Women Returners

Women returners often need re-training before they return to the workplace. Even when they have worked for a reasonable length of time before having a career break, they suffer a loss of confidence. This can come from not knowing how they match up with other job applicants, for their career path shows a number of kinks and unconventional activities (running a home) which potential employers are not used to evaluating. Nor are the women themselves.

But loss of confidence also results from losing touch with the world of work, not knowing how to behave in an environment that has moved on in their absence. This problem is exacerbated if they have a subject specialism which has developed rapidly, like science or engineering, and they need to catch up with the changes before they can be taken seriously as job applicants. Re-training schemes must therefore address the general loss of confidence and also provide facilities for updating knowledge and techniques. In some re-training schemes for women returners mentoring is an essential integral component.

City University Professional Updating The Short Courses Unit of City University runs such a scheme. This is a course sponsored by the Training Agency and lasts nine weeks, combining workshops at the university with actual work experience in local companies. All the women, the trainees, already have a degree qualification or equivalent, and have previously worked outside the home. On this course they meet together for workshops on general topics to re-learn how to interact with colleagues and to enable them to present a positive image, dimmed while at home bringing up children or caring for elderly or infirm relatives – self-presentation, cvs, communication skills, assertiveness, conduct in the workplace and the like. But once a week and later on for an entire week, the trainees are individually placed in local companies for work experience or work shadowing so that they can see how the world of work has changed since the last time they were involved. They can thus learn to adapt their knowledge and behaviour to meet the new requirements.

They also have a mentor assigned to them. The mentor is a member of the University staff and is matched with each trainee according to her subject speciality. A would-be trainee for whom a matching mentor cannot be found, cannot be taken on to the course. The mentor is expected to help the trainee with research to update her skills, and provide any other of the mentoring functions mentioned elsewhere. Particular emphasis is laid on counselling, and the mentor is expected to be generally available to help, guide, etc throughout the nine weeks. There is also a specific contact person in the companies which provide the work experience who will generally oversee the work and experience of the trainee. Whether or not that person performs mentoring as well as administrative functions depends on the individual.

Under this scheme the Training Agency pays the fees of the staff of the university and any outside lecturers. The mentors are also paid. The trainees themselves are paid a small training grant and a

159

travel allowance, and may also under certain circumstances receive help with child minding costs.

There should be more of these courses. The women are enabled to update their skills and therefore be even more valuable to our society. They are also introduced to vital new networks of potential employers to whom they can demonstrate their abilities, and whom they can rely on as referees when they seek permanent work. Equally their mentors can act as referees. And the companies concerned get, without salary costs, the services of someone who is both enthusiastic and mature, eager to learn and perform well. Employers may also find themselves being enlightened by the capacity of today's women returners. So everyone wins.

Fellowship Scheme for Women Returners in Science and Engineering This scheme is also for women already qualified, specifically in a science or engineering subject, but needing updating.

> The objective of this scheme is to provide re-training opportunities for qualified women to regain the expertise and self-confidence necessary to conduct advanced research and thereby to regain a position from which they can compete on equal terms for tenured academic posts or senior research posts in universities and industry (Jackson).

Under this scheme women receive a Fellowship which allows them to spend two or three years at a university re-learning their specialism and updating their skills, often on a part-time basis. They spend some time re-training, attending advanced courses etc, after which they undertake a particular project to advance scientific or engineering knowledge. These Fellowships, like the Windsor Fellowship described above, depend (mostly) on sponsorship by industrial concerns, and the projects the Fellows undertake are often of specific (commercial) interest to the sponsoring company as well as to the university at which the Fellowship is held.

The Fellows are provided with a supervisor at the university where they are working. They may also have another supervisor from the sponsoring company who has a particular interest in the projects they are doing. The primary role of both of these supervisors is academic and technical, to help the women re-learn their subject, learn new research techniques and develop their subject. But reports from the women concerned indicate that their supervisors also exercise a mentoring role in helping them to settle in and come to terms with a scientific environment after several years away, generally to regain confidence and to exercise their creative skills once more in the cause of science and society.

Until her untimely death at the age of 54 in January 1991, Professor Daphne Jackson, Head of the Department of Physics at Surrey University, was the prime mover behind this scheme, initiating it, constantly seeking sponsors, finding suitable universities to take the Fellows, etc. She was officially called the Coordinator, but her role was very much wider than this, embracing virtually all the mentoring functions, from boosting morale to opening career doors. She herself stressed the need to offer counselling, helping the women establish realistic immediate and long-term goals, helping them find a balance between work and domestic responsibilities, negotiating the personality switch between scientist and washer-up, etc. And she often had to give very practical help, for example, to women who have forgotten how to write a CV or present a credible project proposal.

The women participating in the scheme have all found it very valuable, and have obtained decent jobs at the end. Many of them stress the welcome and help that they have been given by their new colleagues, mostly men. But they also underline the benefits of establishing contact (networking) with women from other disciplines in the universities in which they held their Fellowships to share experiences and provide mutual support. Their personal experiences have been reported in a small booklet by Jackson and McCormick.

CHAPTER 8

Setting Up Mentoring and Networking Schemes

In my research for this book I came across women who had benefitted from being mentored informally, but who also wished that a
formal scheme could be established in their company. This is
important not only to the individual employees but to the company
as a whole.

Companies who run development schemes in which mentoring
plays a part reported several benefits which impinge directly on the
profit level of the company. Greater loyalty and lower staff
turnover obviously cut down on personnel costs, but they also
make for better group cohesion and higher productivity, which
increases income. Less easily quantifiable but still vital to profit
levels is the effect on recruitment. A mentoring scheme attracts
people anxious to get ahead, for they then know that their talents
will be sought and nurtured.

Companies who have sponsored students at university and provided them with a mentor during this time say the same thing.
Mentoring shows that the company cares about the staff and is
concerned to get the very best out of them, for mutual profit. It
helps to humanise the workplace, allowing people to find their feet
more quickly and make a significant contribution faster, within the
culture practised by that particular organisation.

Although I am quite certain that these factors are significant for
all staff (although they might not admit it for fear of being called
sissy) they are of admitted interest particularly to women. And
since women will be coming (back) into the workforce more and
more, making up for some of the skills shortages that the demographic dip is revealing, it makes sense for companies to consider
introducing formal mentoring schemes into their staff develop-

ment policy and practice. Indeed BP, a company which has had a major rethink about its policy with regard to developing and using the talents of women staff, has a mentoring component in its retainer schemes to help women on a career break keep in touch with company developments (see Jackson, Margaret).

Setting Up a Mentoring Scheme

Mentoring can form part of recruitment, induction, development and retainer schemes. The suitability of schemes will vary from company to company, but the mentoring schemes described in the last chapter should prove useful as models. But whatever system is chosen a few fundamental issues have to be addressed.

What do you want mentoring to do for your company? Is it realistic? Any new scheme is going to take time before it shows positive results. How long are you prepared to give it? And how are you going to measure the results? Does your company philosophy believe that the happiness of its staff is important in absolute terms, or must everything be immediately and directly quantifiable before it is promoted?

If you think mentoring stands a realistic chance in your company, then ask yourself whether mentoring has top-level approval. If not, forget it. Mentoring, whether promoted or tolerated within a company, requires top-level approval for both policy and practice. Resources – people, time and money – have to be allocated, and that has to be supported from the very top.

Assuming you have top-level approval for the policy, you have to answer detailed questions before putting anything into practice:

- Will mentoring be merely tolerated if it occurs informally, or will it be encouraged?
- If it is encouraged, will it be formalised?
- Will it fit in with or replace existing development practices?
- Will mentoring support a set development programme, or will it stand alone as a person-to-person development tool?
- What will mentors and mentees expect of each other? Should there be a mentoring contract?
- To whom can mentor, mentee or others turn if things go wrong?

- How will problems of resentment and fear of change be handled?
- How long should mentoring from any one mentor last?
- Should there be a recommended pattern of mentoring?
- How will the scheme be monitored and assessed? By whom?
- What administrative support will be needed and provided?
- Who will act as mentors? Will they volunteer or be chosen?
- Who will do the choosing?
- Will mentors be trained?
- Will mentors be assessed on their mentoring? If so, how?
- Should mentoring be part of the job description?
- How should time be allocated to mentoring?
- How should mentoring be rewarded?
- Who will be eligible to be mentored? Everyone by choice, or only those nominated?
- Who will nominate them?
- How will mentors and mentees be matched?
- Who will match them?
- Will mentoring be one-to-one, or one-to-many?

The list above is not exhaustive, but it gives some idea of the kind of careful consideration that should be given to introducing such a powerful development tool as mentoring into a company.

Networks and Mentoring

And, although the environment is different, women's networks thinking about setting up mentoring schemes should go through the same procedure to make sure that they get the most out of mentoring. As a result of your deliberations you may decide that you do not need to set up a formal mentoring scheme, for some women claim to be happy with the kind of networking-mentoring that is possible in women's groups. Indeed some find it a more attractive option than the 'grooming' model of mentoring that we have described in various organisations, feeling that they can in this way engage in more (and probably shorter) mentoring relationships, deriving experience from people of different backgrounds, and being exposed to a wide range of role models.

One of my most helpful respondents claims particular benefit from this type of mentoring from network colleagues. She has never had a 'grooming mentor' in her place of work, but she has had lots of mentoring relationships, some of them lasting over many years, and given and taken in equal measure. I caught up with her recently after a gap of a year and saw her in action mentoring her students of information technology. Not bad for someone who left school without A levels.

Networking-mentoring is similar to peer-mentoring where people of similar status mentor each other in a more or less structured system. And the term 'collegial mentoring' means much the same thing (see Swoboda and Millar). I don't really care what it is called and how it is structured, as long as women learn to get mutual benefit from other people in career terms in whatever system they choose.

Setting Up a Women's Network

In principle the same thing applies to setting up a networking scheme as a mentoring scheme. The first question to ask is whether it is necessary. Are there any existing networks that you could join which would suit your purposes, but save you the administrative bother? If not, you have to write a checklist of questions similar to the ones above, starting with what the unique feature of your network is to be, and who will want to join you in membership. After you have answered those two questions positively, you can go through the list of network features described in Chapter Two and see which you want to incorporate into your new network, and how you will achieve this.

Company Networks

With the growing self-awareness of women at work and their recognition and statement of their development needs to reach senior positions, more and more women's networks are being set up in companies. I want to encourage this, but I also want to add a note of warning. Be very sensitive about the way you handle this. By very definition, if women get more seniority and therefore more power, men lose power. Whilst men often recognise at the intellectual level the justice of this, they are nevertheless emotionally afraid of the consequences. Do try to enlist the support of the men in your company if you want to set up a women's network, and involve them actively, so that they feel they are in control of the sharing of their own power. Otherwise you will encounter suspicion at best and hostility and disruption at worst.

One of the best ways of avoiding this is to get the positive approval of senior (probably male) management in proposing and developing your ideas. Once the chief executive understands the advantages to the company of having more highly trained and promoted women on board, his (sorry) support can be invaluable.

In some companies resources are allocated to support a women's network: the company helps in producing newsletters and publicity, subsidises printing costs, provides postage, allows time off for administrative purposes, provides speakers for workshops, etc. It all depends on how you handle it.

Do also be sensitive about treading on the toes of existing unions or personnel and training departments. Make it quite clear to them that you are not poaching on their traditional territory. They can also be very supportive once they know what you are doing and why, and how, indeed it can further their purposes.

Swan Song

And so we come to the end. I have told you how I think women can improve their chances of getting power in our society by learning to use other people in positive and mutually supportive ways, extending their skills of giving and taking to the employment context. And we need that power to make the work environment more hospitable to the next generation of women (and men). 'We would all like organizations to be nurturing, supportive places, and someday they may be. This may be the greatest contribution that women can bring to work places' (Collins, p86). And we must make the whole world a better place for generations to come, for we shall be judged by the use we make of our power in the workplace. May our mentors give us the strength to act wisely.

APPENDIX I

Dispelling Any Doubts

Many people have contributed to the research for this book. Most of them support networking and mentoring as ways of helping women to achieve success at work. But some have raised a few doubts, which I want to try and dispel here.

Self-Development and Mentoring

Some people object to mentoring in the workplace because they claim that it takes away personal responsibility for one's own development. They say that the only way you can make it in the business world is to be tough and self-reliant, and not depend on others to help you up the ladder. They extend this to claim that you should go it alone and not ask for help from others. In this connection they often use the term 'self-development'. There are two things at issue here: the first is the confusion about the use of the term; the second is a misunderstanding of the nature of mentoring.

'Self-development' is used in at least two ways. It is used to label certain types of training programme. These may be for general consumption, dealing with personal growth and the path through life. Or they may relate to a specific subject or company, and be devised specially for people working in that area. These latter programmes are based on a thorough analysis of the skills and experience that employees need to progress through the company. They are carefully constructed and often very detailed, specifying not only the skills, etc. required, but suggesting the courses, study techniques, work experience, examination work, etc. that will guide the employees in their efforts. The reason that some of these programmes are labelled 'self-development' is that they can be 'self-administered', meaning that the employees can work through them themselves without the supervision of a tutor. Using a degree of common sense, they can tackle the programmes in their own time, at their own pace, in their own way. But it should be noted that some of these programmes make provision for development tutors or 'mentors', or they suggest that it is easier to work through them if you do it with other people.

'Self-development' is also used in connection with people who have not had much formal education, who are largely self-taught, 'autodidacts' in other words. But even then they have often consulted others, or benefitted from the advice of others, about what to read, how to study, what courses to follow, etc.

Self-development therefore does not mean necessarily going it alone. What it does mean is taking personal responsibility for your own development and growth towards certain goals and taking control of how you get there. This implies that you personally determine what your goals are, and that you map out a route to follow, and set a number of intermediary targets to reach on the way. It also implies that you will determine what you use to help you. You have a variety of learning resources at your disposal, books, courses, other people.

And these other people of course include mentors. Self-development therefore leaves up to you whether you use the services of a personal guide on your route to your goal, in the same way that you can choose to rely on a map, a company programme, or not. It certainly does not necessitate doing away with mentors.

And the nature of mentoring is not in any case such that personal responsibility is taken away from you. Even if you have a mentor who is very pro-active in the help and advice she gives you, this does not take from you the responsibility for accepting (or rejecting) her support. She may present you with learning opportunities, but only you can do the learning. She may open doors for you, but only you can walk through them. The most she, or the organisation, can do is facilitate your progress. But you remain responsible for you. As an adult human being, you are responsible for developing yourself.

Elitism

Another reason why people feel uncomfortable about mentoring is that they consider it elitist and therefore unacceptable in today's world. They say we should be promoting people according to their ability and not because of their connections with, or membership of, some small favoured group.

I have some sympathy with this view, if by elitism is meant the promotion of an individual with connections which have nothing to do with the capacity to do the job. This can work exclusively, disqualifying people from promotion if they are not members of a certain group, for example, the male group of our society. Or it can happen inclusively, as when Jill Jones is preferred to Sara Smith merely because she is Lord Jones's daughter. (It is difficult to see at first glance how her close connections with the Establishment guarantee her qualities as a geological engineer.) In such cases promoting on the basis of connections is a nonsense and a dangerous nonsense, for it prevents the best person from being appointed, and our economy is not such that it will permit such folly for very much longer.

If on the other hand Jill Jones is preferred because a trusted friend of your company (Lord Jones) has known her for years and recommends the quality of her work, while Sara Smith is apparently equally well-qualified but unknown to the selectors, or the people whose judgement of work suitability they trust, then that is an entirely different kettle of fish.

What is wrong here is not the connections, but the relevance of the connections. One of my reasons for writing this book is that I want women to appreciate the importance of connections. I want to help them to develop their own so that they are not passed over time and again because they haven't got the right ones. I want them to get themselves into positions where they *do* connect with the people able to influence their promotion, so that their competence can be seen, and they will be promoted because they are known to be the right person for the job. And as we have seen, both networking and mentoring are important in doing this.

Where mentoring can be elitist is in the failure of the mentors or the mentoring scheme to make the right choice of mentee, excluding members of some groups, or including only members of some groups. For example, I do not care for the situation where mentoring is restricted to those judged to be high performers or (very) fast trackers when they enter a company, and where entry to the mentoring scheme is virtually impossible thereafter. This does not allow for later development, and given the advantages that mentoring can bring, it is grossly unfair to those who were not picked, and who may have developed as well or better with some personal attention.

Favouritism

This is also a form of elitism, but has less to do with group connections than personal ones. For reasons which we cannot always fathom, an individual is liked by someone in a position of influence and given special treatment, either in opportunity or reward. This happens with the teacher's pet, the child whom the teacher likes especially, and who gets prestigious tasks to perform, conferring a power which the others find unjustified, and which they resent.

And favouritism also happens, for more obvious reason, with the son of the owner of the business. Even if he is sent to start on the floor of the factory, he is supervised and guided, given personal tuition, provided with work shadowing in every part of the company until he is able to step into daddy's shoes. He may, to do him justice, be very suitable to step into his father's shoes. But so might other people be if they had been encouraged and groomed (mentored) in the same way.

What therefore is elitist about mentoring is the inadequate selection of mentees, not the nature of the training itself. This can stop the best people from reaching the top, and be unfair to those not selected, causing resentment, reduced productivity and resignation from the company.

Equal Opportunities

I know a Director of Equal Opportunities who is very concerned about the apparent elitism, therefore lack of equality of opportunity, of mentoring. The irony of this is that she works in a company which has a highly structured personal development programme which includes mentoring as a major component. She explains this inconsistency by saying that anyone in her company can apply to go on the development programme, so everyone has an equal opportunity to be mentored. When I object that in theory this is true, but in practice not everyone is equally encouraged to apply, she becomes very tight-lipped.

Most of my life has been spent in encouraging equality of opportunity in education and employment, and I shall go to my grave still fighting for it. So I regret having to say that I think a lot of the equal opportunities policies I know about do not in practice give women (or the other groups they are meant to protect) any more equal opportunity, and indeed in many cases hamper them. To be fair, I think they often hamper very suitable men, too.

Another of life's little ironies is that 'equal opportunities selection procedures' were introduced in large part to obviate the abuses of informal networks where 'jobs for the boys' was the order of the day. It is fine for networks or mentors to produce boys for the job, but only if the best 'boys' are produced. And often they have not been. In which case the organisation suffers, the employees, the customers and the shareholders. In an attempt to overcome the iniquities of systems which allowed mentors or other network contacts to appoint their own, rather than the best person available, unions and management in Britain have codified and standardised certain policies and procedures. These include job evaluation, salaries and grading, promotion and appointment.

Under the system which has emerged all jobs in the organisations concerned must be advertised publicly. There is no internal promotion and uncompetitive redeployment is rare. The job advertisement specifies what criteria will be sought in the applicants, and all applicants with those criteria must be interviewed. The procedure for the interview usually specifies that the same questions shall be asked of each candidate, and the interviewers have 'ideal' answers in their minds which will allow them to select the most suitable candidate. This system was devised to avoid discrimination on the grounds of gender, age, ethnic origin, religion and disability. But in practice it is proving unsatisfactory: it fails to allow the candidate a free input into the discussion, forbids the interviewers to pursue a point (no matter how interesting and relevant) made by one candidate because they were not able to pursue that point with an earlier candidate who did not raise the point, etc. And it does not allow the interviewers to judge whether the applicant would fit in well with existing staff.

There are three things wrong with this system of interviewing. Firstly, the system is based on a job analysis, and rarely takes into account how that job fits in with equal and higher positions. The interviewers are therefore constrained to appoint someone for her match with the job criteria specified, rather than her longer-term suitability for work with the company.

Secondly, the system also assumes that background is irrelevant. I strongly contest this. People arrive at a similar point (in this case job applications) from different routes in life, and the route they have taken, the hurdles they have overcome, the guidance they have received on the way, all affect how they will operate in future. Some will prefer to follow guidelines, others will be more individually creative in the way they help the company grow. Such distinctions cannot be revealed by a questioning technique that assumes sameness, and therefore uniqueness of right answer. If interviewers are stopped from saying, 'That is very interesting. Why did you say that?' then the information on which they judge is severely limited.

Thirdly, the system officially excludes a fit with company culture. If a machine is to operate properly all parts of it must mesh together. If one part grates against the others, in other words, disturbs the company culture, then the machine won't work properly, inefficiency results, and the delivery of goods and services suffers. Except in very few cases it is impossible to appoint properly to a job without considering the whole person of the candidate and the people environment to which you are appointing.

This system really has to go back to the drawing board, for it doesn't get the right people. Many good people have been rejected in favour of the mundane. In any case it doesn't work in its own terms of appointing only the people who fit the criteria stated. The application forms still ask for background information which reveals how people attained the criteria for the job; they still ask for the names of referees; they still ask internal candidates to specify their line manager as one referee. Referees, particularly line managers, are bound to give information about the suitability of candidates to work and progress in the environment, including how well they will fit in with other staff. In other words, the system does allow for the influence of network contacts and mentors, even though it claims it doesn't. It is in the nature of human beings to take the people factor into account. And if any system tries not to, it is doomed to fail.

I am all for a situation which excludes pointless discrimination, and that is why I am writing this book – to enable women to develop their potential, make an important contribution to our society and get a fair slice of the cake in return. And I think networking and mentoring are pretty powerful ways of encouraging their development. Undoubtedly abuses of networking and mentoring do occur, but the system outlined above won't stop them. Its greatest merit is that equal opportunities advertisements make it clear that applications from women are welcome. But if the selection criteria then exclude the strengths of women's cultures, what chance do they have?

Back-Door Entry

There is another objection that women in particular seem to have to networking and mentoring. They see it as the back-door way of gaining entry. Their first reaction is that this is gate-crashing. The use of this term implies that they are entering territory where they don't belong. When I ask ingenuously why they don't belong, they produce their second reaction: that this is a second-class citizen's route and they want to go through the front door, doing it publicly on the basis of competence alone. What they don't realise is that most of the people who do it through the front door have benefitted from precisely the kind of help that networking and mentoring bring. Only they don't talk about it, because for them it is so much part of their way of life that it is not worthy of comment.

I also have to say that there often isn't a front door in the sense that women would want there to be. They want a situation in which the rules are known, and all they have to do is obey the rules to be rewarded. But life isn't like that, despite the very best intentions of equal opportunities policies. Jobs in the private sector do not have to be advertised, and many are not, so a front door does not exist. In many of the large companies that I have interviewed for this book they say that they prefer to grow their own. They want to promote from within if at all possible, so that they know where they are with the 'new' person. Even in smaller companies there is often someone who is 'bringing someone on' or who knows just the person who will be right for what they have in mind. So it is the back door or not at all.

Masculine Behaviour

A further objection is that mentoring and networking are particularly male activities. I have two replies to this. The first I have already discussed, namely that women are very good at networking, finding out who and what can meet their private needs and the needs of their family; but they do not naturally transfer this to the workplace, for they do not naturally feel this to be their territory where their rules operate.

My second reply is that what happens in the workplace is not necessarily male. It is often called so because males are statistically dominant in the workplace. But that does not mean that they have any kind of prerogative on certain characteristics and behaviour patterns. Women mentor too, but again on the domestic front, or in charitable work. Their goals are different but in principle the techniques and mutual advantages are the same. Some of us have transferred these techniques to our workplace without any trouble at all and want to help others to do so.

Aping Men

My reply to this objection is the same as in the paragraph above. But I would add another reply, and that is this: so what? I think it is nonsense not to do something merely because men do it. Certainly we women have many characteristics, traditionally viewed as female, from which the workplace could benefit (see Sargent, and Bryce), but that should not stop us from using or adopting others. My attitude is, if it is efficient, and it doesn't harm anyone, then do it.

Back-Scratching

I respond in similar fashion to the comment that networking and mentoring are just mutual back-scratching. Who is harmed by it? I encourage it so that more people can benefit. If someone is harmed, if someone is left out, then that is a reason for improving the system, not discarding it.

Resentment

Some staff feel resentment about the rate at which people who are mentored make progress. They fall into two groups.

173

Unmentored Senior Staff

The first ones are to be found among those senior people the company would want to use as mentors. They say that they had to get to the top the hard way without any help, so why should the newcomers expect help to be handed to them on a plate? This happens particularly with managers who have not been to university who are expected to mentor graduates, or managers without an MBA expected to mentor MBAS. They say that the newcomers already have advantage enough with their university education and professional qualifications. Now they should get down to proving their ability, rather than expecting further spoon-feeding.

This is not easy to handle. There are plenty of reasons why they could be feeling resentful. Perhaps they did have a hard time, and perhaps they genuinely feel that their struggle to overcome their difficulties was what brought them their success, and that that is the best way to do it. This is the self-reliant syndrome noted above. Or perhaps they are jealous of the younger people, of their 'gifts' of the education that has come their way, and the 'ease' with which they have made their way in the world. The senior people had to achieve their status as a result of a lot of hard work, and here they are now being expected to teach everything they have ever learned to young kids who have 'bought' their seniority by a university education. If this is what they feel, telling them that getting a degree is hard work is pointless. If they have an emotional hang-up about this, no amount of intellectual discussion is going to convince them.

But one of the most likely reasons for their resentment is that they feel threatened by the younger whizz-kids, particularly if they are younger whizz-girls. For then they are dealing not only with younger versions of traditional heroes who are rising faster than the heroes, but a different category of hero who has suddenly and unexpectedly appeared on the stage and whose characteristics are unknown. And this applies to senior men or women. The shock to the system is great. They see their seniority disappearing in months as these young things have a chance to demonstrate their calibre in the company. And where will they be then when their years of experience count for nothing any more?

Certainly forcing them to take part in mentoring won't help. An appeal to company loyalty might make them toe the line, but it will not make a good mentor out of an unwilling one. Probably the best way to handle this is to talk to the whizz-kids themselves, and get them to understand how important the contribution is that X and Y make to the company, and how they will be able to get on very much faster if they seek their advice and follow their example. In this way, the youngsters themselves can, by their actions, convince the older ones that experience and maturity still have an important place in their work for the company, both through their continuing operational activities and through the accumulated wisdom that they can pass on. X and Y may in time remember the number of people who will have given them a helping hand over the years, and they may lose their apprehension about helping others. They may even begin to enjoy all the benefits that mentoring bright young people brings.

Unmentored Junior Staff

The second group to express resentment is found amongst those junior staff who have not been mentored. Such group resentment can be power-ful, and can bring about the downfall of the mentoring pair. I was told of one particularly sad story. A (male) manager who was head of his depart-ment took as his mentee a young female trainee. Her rise was rapid, and there was little doubt that this was due, at least in part, to his mentoring. He was an international authority in their field and he opened doors for her at home and abroad. Together they went to conferences and presen-ted joint papers. She was even sent on foreign study trips which consider-ably broadened her experience. And when he went on a long foreign assignment, she went too.

This was strongly resented by other staff who did not get what was considered 'special treatment'. Whether they were having a sexual affair was not clear, but this was generally held to be the case, and did not make either of them well-liked. So strong was this view that, when the wife of the mentor also went on foreign trips with them, it was assumed that she was merely being used to distract from the truth.

In the end his luck ran out, and he was obliged to leave the company. But so was she. She had no one in the department or the company who could trust her to do the job without his back-up. She had got herself in a position where she couldn't be judged on her own merits.

One of the major things that had gone wrong was the failure of both of them to look after their other colleagues. Although he was respected as an authority in his field, he was not liked. He was both rude and self-seeking, showed no respect for other people, and did nothing to help others unless they were useful to him. So nobody was going to do much to support his attempts to stay with the company. She was a gentle person, but failed to network properly with her peer colleagues – those who were not mentored – associating rarely with them, working only with him. She expected little of her peers, and got little in return. Had she spent more time with them, they might have understood that she really was good in her own right and deserved the promotion she was getting. And they might not have resen-ted her so much.

In short, mentoring can cause resentment, but the damaging effects on the morale of other staff can be controlled.

In Summary

Many of the objections noted above stem from the consequences of the notorious worst form of networking where people have been given jobs (for which they were often unsuitable, and thereby unjustly excluding suitable people) just because they belong to the right networks, right school, right universities, OBN, Mafia, Freemasons, etc. where mutual favours are given and expected. (See Müller-Mees for a German angle on the same problem.) Or because women have in the past had to provide for the influential people of this world the kind of service most often delivered on the office couch, before they are given decent jobs. Clearly I condemn that as firmly as my vocabulary allows. Not only because of my distaste for the attitudes thereby revealed, but because of the consequences for other women.

> Women can't use the business world as an emotional or a sexual playground and succeed; it will mark them forever as 'just women' when what they want is to be taken seriously for the good things they have to offer. For every woman who . . . screws her way up the ladder, another will get screwed (Collins, p50).

But do not let us throw the baby out with the bath water. Let us rather take from these systems the features that are good and use them to our advantage, and to that of the nation.

Appendix II

Women's Organisations and Campaigns

Belgravia Breakfast Club
c/o Sheraton Park Tower Hotel, 101 Knightsbridge, London SW1X 7RN.
Tel: 071-235 8050

City Women's Network
925 Uxbridge Road, Hillingdon Heath, Middx UB10 0NJ.
Tel: 081-569 2351

European Association of Professional Secretaries (EAPS)
Barbara Smith, Secretary, Heathrow Business Centre, Terminal 2,
Heathrow Airport, Hounslow, Middx TW6 1EU. Tel: 071-371 2443

European Network of Women (UK Section)
Anne M. McGlone, 52–54 Featherstone Street, London EC2V 8RT.
Tel: 071-720 9382

European Women's Management Development Network
c/o 27 Brewer Street, Brighton, BN2 3HH. Tel: 0273 686652

Forum UK
83 St George's Road, London SE1 6ER. Tel: 071-582 3916

National Alliance of Women's Organisations (NAWO)
279/281 Whitechapel Road, London E1 1BY. Tel: 071-247 7052

Network
9 Abbotts Yard, 35 King Street, Royston, Herts SG8 9AZ.
Tel: 0763 242225

Townswomen's Guild (TG)
Chamber of Commerce House, 75 Harborne Road, Birmingham
B15 3DA. Tel: 021-456 3435

UK Federation of Business and Professional Women (UKBPW)
23 Ansdell Street, Kensington, London W8 5BN. Tel: 071-938 1729

177

Women and Training (London)
c/o CSA, 15 Harwood Road, London SW6 4QP. Tel: 071-736 6975

Women in Banking
c/o Caroline Gaffney, NatWest, 166 Camden High Street, London NW1 0NS. Tel: 071-485 7121

Women in BP
Britannic House, Moor Lane, Moorgate, London EC2 9BU.
Tel: 071-920 3896

Women in Computing
Lorna Uden, Campaign Director, Staffordshire Polytechnic, College Road, Stoke-on-Trent, Staffs ST4 2DE. Tel: 0782 744531

Women in Higher Education Network (WHEN)
King's College, Cambridge CB2 1ST. Tel: 0223 350411

Women in Information Technology (WIT)
Phillip Virgo, Campaign Director, c/o IT Strategy Services, 2 Eastbourne Avenue, London W3 6JN. Tel: 081-992 3575

Women in Management (WIM)
64 Marryat Road, Wimbledon, London SW19 5BN. Tel: 081-944 6332

Women into Public Life (WIPL)
c/o 110 Riverview Gardens, London SW13 9RA. Tel: 081-748 1427

Women into Science and Engineering (WISE)
Mr Shillito, Head of Centre, TICST, Trent Polytechnic, Burton Street, Nottingham NG1 4BU. Tel: 0602 418418

Women's Engineering Society
c/o Eugenie Maxwell, Imperial College of Science and Technology, Dept. of Civil Engineering, Imperial College Road, London SW7 2BU.
Tel: 071-589 5111, Ext. 4731

300 Group
36–37 Charterhouse Square, London EC1M 6EA. Tel: 071-600 2390

300 Group Educational Trust
c/o 4 Slayleigh Avenue, Sheffield S10 3RB. Tel: 0742 304098

A directory of more than 150 women's organisations is produced by:
Women's National Commission (WNC), Cabinet Office, Government Offices, Horse Guards Road, London SW1P 3AL. Tel: 071-270 5903

APPENDIX III

Mentoring Schemes

Fellowship Scheme for Women Returners to Science and Engineering
c/o Department of Physics, University of Surrey, Guildford GU2 5XH.
Tel: 0483 509 166

Guardian Angel Scheme
Institute of Translation and Interpreting, 318a Finchley Road, London
NW3 5HT. Tel: 071-794 9931

Mentor Project
c/o Howard Jeffrey, North London College, 444 Camden Road, London
N7 0SP. Tel: 071-609 9981

Professional Updating for Women
Short Course Unit, City University, Northampton Square, London
EC1V 0HB. Tel: 071-490 2832

Windsor Fellowship
c/o Citicorp, 336 Strand, London WC2R 1HB. Tel: 071-438 1056

BIBLIOGRAPHY

Arnold, Vivienne, 'Women and Mentoring', *Women Managers' Network*, Issue no. 2, summer 1989, pp1–2.

Arnold, Vivienne, and **Davidson**, Marilyn J., 'Adopt a Mentor – The New Way Ahead for Women Managers?', *Women in Management Review and Abstracts*, vol. 5, no. 1, 1990, pp1–18.

Balsdon, Diana, 'The National Westminster Bank' in Currie, Edwina, *qv*.

BIM, 'Creating a Committed Workforce', Proceedings of the Second National Conference, London, 1984, pp5–6.

BIM, *Mentoring*, MINT Series, 1987.

Bowen, Donald D., 'Were Men Meant to Mentor Women?' *Training and Development Journal*, USA, February 1985, pp31–34.

Bryce, Lee, *The Influential Woman*, Piatkus Books, London, 1989.

Burnard, Philip, 'A Supporting Act', *Nursing Times*, London, 16–22 November 1988, pp27–28.

Carter, Sara, and **Cannon**, Tom, *Women in Business*, Scottish Enterprise Foundation, November 1988.

Clawson, James G., 'Is Mentoring Necessary?', *Training and Development Journal*, USA, April 1985, pp36–39.

Clutterbuck, David, *Everyone Needs a Mentor: How to Foster Talent within an Organisation*, Institute of Personnel Management, London, 1985.

Clutterbuck, David, 'Skills without Spills: A New Way', *The Times*, 14 February 1985, p27.

Clutterbuck, David, and **Devine**, Marion (eds), *Businesswoman: Present and Future*, Macmillan, London, 1987.

Clutterbuck, David, and **Devine**, Marion, 'Having a Mentor: A Help or a Hindrance?' in Clutterbuck and Devine, *qv*.

Colback, Sharon, and **Maconochie**, Michael, 'In the Vanguard of the Revolution', *The Sunday Times Magazine*, London, 4 February 1990.

Collin, A., 'Mentoring', *Industrial and Commercial Training*, March/April 1988, 20/2, pp23–27.

Collins, Eliza G. C., *Dearest Amanda: An Executive's Advice to Her Daughter*, Harper & Row, New York, 1984.

Collins, Eliza G. C., and **Scott**, Patricia, 'Everyone who Makes it has a Mentor', *Harvard Business Review*, July/August 1978, vol. 56, No. 4, pp89–101.

Currie, Edwina, and others, *What Women Want*, Sidgwick & Jackson, London, 1990.

Dalton, G. W., **Thompson**, P. H., and **Price**, R. L., 'The Four Stages of Professional Careers', *Organisational Dynamics*, summer 1977, pp19–42.

Daloz, L. A., *Effective Teaching and Mentoring*, Jossey-Bass, London, 1986.

Davidson, Marilyn, *Reach for the Top*, Piatkus Books, London, 1985.

Devine, Marion, 'Receiving a Helping Hand', *Self-development*, The ITEM Group Ltd, Bucks, August 1987, pp5–7.

Dix, Carol. *A Chance for the Top: The Lives of Women Business Graduates*, Bantam Press, London, 1990.

English National Board of Nursing, ENB(89)17.

Farren, C., **Dreyfus Gray**, J., and **Kaye**, B., 'Mentoring: A Boon to Career Development', *Personnel*, November/December 1984, pp20–24.

Firth-Cozens, J., and **West**, Michael, *Women at Work: Psychological and Organisational Perspectives*, Open University Press, Milton Keynes, 1990.

Gallagher, Elaine, 'Snap Up a Mentor', *Guide to Success*, a supplement of *Cosmopolitan* magazine in association with Reed Employment, April 1987.

Graham, Pauline, *Dynamic Managing – the Follett Way*, British Institute of Management, Professional Publishing Ltd, London, 1987.

Grant, Jane, *Sisters Across the Atlantic: A Guide to Networking in the US*, NCVO, 1988.

Gray, Marilyn Miles (ed), 'Mentoring and Coaching – An Annotated Bibliography', *Mentoring International*, vol. 3, no. 4, Vancouver, autumn 1989.

Hammond, V., 'Reviewing Your Training Practices in a Positive Way', in Richardson and Davidson, *qv*.

Harvey-Jones, John, *Making it Happen: Reflections on Leadership*, Collins, London, 1988.

Heald, Tim, *Networks: Who We Know and How We Use Them*, Hodder and Stoughton, London, 1983.

Healy, Madelyn, 'Designing a Mentoring Program for First-Year College Faculty', *South African Journal of Higher Education*, vol. 3, no. 2, 1987.

Hennig, Margaret, and **Jardim**, Anne, *The Managerial Woman*, Pan Books, London, 1979.

Hertz, Leah, *Business Amazons*, Methuen, London, 1987.

Hetherington, Cheryl, and **Barcelo**, Rusty, 'Womentoring: A Cross-Cultural Perspective', *Journal of NAWDAC*, fall 1985, pp12–15.

Honoria, *The Female Mentor: or Selected Conversations*, vols. 1–3, 1793–96.

Hunt, D. M., and **Michael**, C., 'Mentorship: A Career Training and Development Tool', Academy of Management Review, vol. 8, no. 3, 1983.

Industrial Society and Item Group, *The Line-Manager's Role in Developing Talent*, Conference Proceedings available from the Industrial Society.

Jack, Andrew, 'Power and Muscle from an Extra Brain', *Financial Times*, 15 January 1990, p10.

Jackson, Daphne F., 'Problems Facing Qualified Women Returners', in Firth-Cozens and West, *qv.*

Jackson, Daphne F., and **McCormick**, Elizabeth, *Fellowship Scheme for Women Returners to Science and Engineering: Personal Experiences*, University of Surrey, Guildford, 1988.

Jackson, Margaret, 'British Petroleum', in Currie, Edwina, *qv.*

Jarvie, David, and **Matthews**, Jack, 'A Counselling Approach to Development Management', *Training and Development*, London, August 1989, pp9–10.

Kochan, Nick, 'Guidance along the Jungle Trail', *The Times*, 10 May 1989, pI, Section 3.

Kram, Kathy E., 'Phases of the Mentor Relationship', *Academy of Management Journal*, December 1983, pp608–625.

Kram, Kathy E., *Mentoring at Work: Developmental Relationships in Organisational Life*, Scott Foresman, London, 1985.

Kram, Kathy E., 'Improving the Mentoring Process', *Training and Development Journal*, USA, April 1985, pp40–43.

Laurent, Claire, 'On Hand to Help', *Nursing Times*, London, 16–22 November 1988, pp29–30.

Lawton, Denis, and **Gordon**, Peter, *HMI*, Routledge & Kegan Paul, London, 1987.

Lean, Elizabeth, 'Cross-Gender Mentoring: Downright Upright and Good for Productivity', *Training and Development Journal*, USA, May 1983, pp61–65.

Leigh, Andrew, 'Creative Partners', *Training and Development*, London, August 1989, p8.

LGTB, Local Government Training Board, *Training Package for the Development of Mentors*, ref. no. ED0012, 1985.

Lyles, Marjorie A., 'Strategies for Helping Women Managers – or Anyone', *Personnel*, January/February 1983, pp67–77.

Macdonald, Eleanor, *Nothing by Chance!* Nimrod Press Ltd, Hants, 1988.

Mcdonald, Janet W., *Climbing the Ladder: How to be a Woman Manager*, Methuen-Mandarin, London, 1989 (original edition 1986).

McKeen, C. A., and **Burke**, R. J., 'Mentor Relationships in Organizations', *The Journal of Management Development* (UK), vol. 8, no. 6, 1989, p33.

Marshall, Judi, *Women Travellers in a Male World*, John Wiley and Sons Ltd, 1984.

Megginson, David, 'Instructor, Coach, Mentor: Three Ways of Helping for Managers', *Management Education and Development*, vol. 19, part 1, 1988, pp34–46.

Morle, Kate, 'Patterns, Progress and Potential', paper read to Directors of Nurse Education Annual Conference 1988, Royal College of Nursing.

Morris, Nigel, **John**, Glynn, and **Keen**, Tom, 'Mentors, Learning the Ropes', *Nursing Times*, London, 16–22 November 1988, pp24–27.

Müller-Mees, Elke, *Was heisst schon Männersache!*, Ariston-Verlag, Geneva, 1990.

Mumford, Alan, 'What's New in Management Development', *Personnel Management*, May 1985, pp30–32.

Murray, Hugh, and **Packard**, Peter, 'Training in Coaching Skills', *Training and Development*, London, August 1989, pp11–12.

Myers, Donald W., and **Humphreys**, Neil J., *The Caveats in Mentorship*, Business Horizons, July/August 1985, pp9–14.

NASD, National Association of Staff Development in Further and Higher Education, *Mentorship*, Conference Papers, 1984.

Novarra, Virginia, *Women's Work, Men's Work; The Ambivalence of Equality*, Marion Boyars, London, 1980.

Odiorne, George S., 'Mentoring – An American Management Innovation', *Personnel Administrator*, May 1985, pp63–70.

PA Consulting Group, *Management Development and Mentoring: An International Study*, London, 1986.

Phillips-Jones, Linda, *Mentors and Protégés: How to Establish, Strengthen and Get the Most from a Mentor/Protégé Relationship*, Arbor House, New York, 1982 (not available in UK).

Phillips-Jones, Linda, 'Establishing a Formalised Mentoring Program', *Training and Development*, USA, February 1983, pp33–42.

Reich, Murray H., 'Executive Views from Both Sides of Mentoring', *Personnel*, March 1985, pp42–46.

Reich, Murray H., 'The Mentor Connection', *Personnel*, February 1986, pp50–51.

Richardson, Helen, and **Davidson**, Marilyn J., *Meeting the Training Needs of Your Female Managers*, Manpower Services Commission, 1985.

Robson-Scott, Markie, 'The Best Years of a Girl's Life?', *Guardian* 30 May 1990, p17.

183

Sangster, C. L. G., 'Realities of Developing Managers in an "Average Company" ', *Journal of European and Industrial Training*, vol. 9, 1985, pp17–22.

Sargent, Alice, *The Androgynous Manager*, AMACOM, New York, 1981.

Scott Welch, Mary, *Networking: The Great New Way for Women to Get Ahead*, Harcourt Brace Jovanovich Inc, New York, 1980 (not available in UK).

Sidney, Elizabeth, and **Phillips**, Nicola, *One-to-One Management*, Pitman Publishing, London, 1990.

Slaughter, Audrey, *Your Brilliant Career*, Macdonald Optima, London, 1987.

Stechert, Kathryn, *The Credibility Gap*, Thorson's Publishing Group, 1987 (first published as *Sweet Success*, Macmillan, New York, 1986).

Stechert Black, Kathryn, 'Why It Pays to Have a Mentor', *Working Mother*, McCall's Group, New York, September 1989, pp33–36.

Steele, Maggie, and **Thornton**, Zita, *Women Can Achieve Career Success*, Grapevine, 1988.

Syrett, Michel, 'A Bit of Help on the Way Up the Ladder', *The Sunday Times*, 9 August 1987, p59.

Swoboda, Marion J., and **Millar**, Susan B., 'Networking-Mentoring: Career Strategy of Women in Academic Administration', *Journal of NAWDAC*, fall 1986, pp8–13.

Watson, Sophia, *Winning Women*, Weidenfeld and Nicolson, London, 1989.

Whyte, Alison, 'Images of Success', *Times Educational Supplement*, 8 June 1990, pB2.

Zey, Michael G., *The Mentor Connection*, Dow Jones Irwin, Illinois, 1984.

Zey, Michael G., 'Mentor Programmes: Making the Right Moves', *Personnel Journal*, February 1985, pp53–57.

INDEX